How YOUth
Can
Succeed!

Transforming Dreams
Into Reality for Young Adults

What others are saying about the author and this book...

"Sean is an outrageous young man with great strategies for life."

– Anthony Robbins, Best selling author of *Unlimited Power*

• • • • •

". . . Sean and his desire and genuine care for our youth exemplifies what TRUTH and HONOR are all about. He is a gem in the world of pebbles, and I strongly encourage all young people to not only read this book, but follow his advice. He is a role model and a great source of inspiration."

– Jeff Yalden, Marine of the Year and co-author of *Lead Now...or Get Out of the Way!*

• • • • •

"*How YOU^{th} Can Succeed!* is a treasure that changes lives. I truly believe Sean Stephenson's message is a fountain of inspiration for all those who want to succeed! Sean is the message that he brings, he motivates all of us to manifest our greatness."

– Les Brown, Best selling author of *Live Your Dreams* and *It's Not Over Until You Win*

• • • • •

"You are in for a real treat...Sean knows how to tickle the soul, maximize human potential, and create lasting success. Read this book and then take action!"

– Patricia Fripp, (CSP, CPAE), Author of *Get What You Want*

• • • • •

"...I was both impressed and astounded by his (Sean) exceptional remarks...a grace and brilliance far beyond his years."

– John "Dukes of Hazzard" Schneider, Actor & Musician

• • • • •

"I have known Sean Stephenson since 1996 and everything he has accomplished amazes me. I believe Sean is an outstanding communicator because he knows how to transform knowledge into power for everyone."

– U.S. Rep. William O. Lipinski, Illinois Third District

"This book challenged me to grow and learn in ways I never thought possible. *How YOUth Can Succeed!* is a treasure for young adults and an educator's dream."

– Kary Odiatu (BPE, BEd), Ms. Fitness Universe & author of *Fit for Love*

· · · · ·

"In a lifetime of working with young people, I have not met anyone who exceeds Sean's courage, dedication, and integrity. He is a young man America can be proud of, a leader who will make a difference."

**– Major General Patrick H. Brady (USARET),
Congressional Medal of Honor Receipt**

· · · · ·

"…We all have our challenges. Sean's are obvious at first, but disappear as he engages you. He has something important to share with the rest of us with less obvious challenges."

– Rev. John P. Minogue, C.M., President, DePaul University

· · · · ·

"…Sean leaves an impression that cannot be erased or forgotten. He is a tremendous young man."

– Ronald Engel, Director of American Legion Boys Nation

· · · · ·

"Sean is a leader for our times and this book has his secrets."

– Tad Hargrave, the Global Youth Coach

· · · · ·

"…Sean is not only a wonderful model for young people today but also, I believe, a young leader of tomorrow."

– Richard D. Parker, Williams Professor of Law, Harvard Law School

· · · · ·

"I have never met a more thoughtful and considerate young man than Sean Stephenson. He is a perfect role model for every American teen."

– Daniel S. Wheeler, President of the Citizens Flag Alliance, Inc.

· · · · ·

"Courage escorts him (Sean) everywhere he goes and inspiration is left everywhere he has been."

– Fr. Bill Stenzel, Pastor of Saint Francis Xavier

How YOUth Can Succeed!

Transforming Dreams
Into Reality for Young Adults

Sean C. Stephenson

SCS Publishing
LaGrange, IL

How YOUth Can Succeed!
Transforming Dreams Into Reality for Young Adults

Copyright © 2001 by Sean C. Stephenson

Published by: SCS Publishing
                LaGrange, Illinois

First edition

Front cover photo compliments of S. Stephenson
Back cover photo compliments of Premier Boys State / American Legion
Cover design by Ad Graphics, Inc., Tulsa, Oklahoma
Printed in the United States of America

Stephenson, Sean C.
    How youth can succeed! : transforming dreams
  into reality for young adults / Sean C.
  Stephenson. — 1st ed.
    p. cm.
    LCCN: 00-191696
    ISBN: 0-9703381-0-4

  1. Success. 2. Self-actualization (Psychology).
3. Life skills. I. Title.

BJ1611.2.S84 2000   158.1'083
                   QB100-500145

WARNING:

Reading this book may cause several of the following severe side affects…

- Extremely strong self-confidence!
- Academic enhancement!
- Uncontrollable urges to improve!
- The ability to take charge of your destiny!
- Sore smiling muscles!
- Zero tolerance for procrastination!
- Surges of intense gratitude!
- The destruction of doubt!
- Lasting change!

ABOUT THE AUTHOR

Sean Clinch Stephenson's appearance, accomplishments, attitude, and physical ability are not typical for a young adult. When he was born, the doctors told his parents, he wouldn't even survive the first night. Now, over two decades later, Sean is traveling across the nation working with leaders ranging from student government presidents to the President of the United States. While in high school, Sean entertained television audiences by producing, directing, and writing award-winning talk shows, soap operas, dating games, and political interviews.

Prior to his current involvement in the field of personal development, Sean's focus was government. Being elected out of 1,000 boys to the office of governor (at Illinois Boys State) was an experience that sparked his political curiosity. Following his election to governor, Sean was appointed by the American Legion to represent Illinois in the elite youth organization, Boys Nation, an honor reserved for only 96 individuals out of 38,000. During his education in political science at DePaul University, Sean spent his summers working with the highest officials in the nation's capital. While working for his mentor, Congressman William O. Lipinski, on Capitol Hill, Sean learned about democracy up close and personal. After his experience with Congress, Sean moved on to the executive branch. During his stay at the White House, Sean assisted the President, Vice President, and Cabinet Secretaries as an intern for the Office of Cabinet Affairs. Although politics remains in his heart, Sean's true allegiance is to inspirational speaking and writing.

At an early age, Sean realized his calling was to help people overcome their obstacles and maximize their lives. By the time he was twenty, he had addressed numerous schools, business, hospitals, foundations, and government agencies, including the Federal Aviation Administration (FAA) and the United States Senate on two occasions. As the CEO of his own company, Sean is touching the lives of thousands ranging in age from kindergartners to corporate executives. Sean attributes his own success to both emotional and physical mastery. Sean shares his fitness passion in a series of workout tapes called "NO EXCUSES." The purpose of this series is to motivate both the able and disabled community to make fitness an everyday priority. Sean most definitely has far surpassed societies' expectations of a physically-challenged youth. This is because everyday he defies the odds of his rare bone disorder, Osteogenesis Imperfecta, which has stunted his growth, caused his bones to be brittle (fracturing over 200 times), and limited his mobility to a wheelchair.

Visit Sean online at: **www.seanstephenson.com**.

DEDICATION

*To all those individuals who are
committed to improving the world:
May you recognize that first you need
to improve yourself.*

ACKNOWLEDGMENTS

Thank you, Mom, Dad, Heidi, and my extended family, you are the reason I survived my voyage to the *Kingdom of Success*.

CHAPTERS FOR SUCCESS

FOREWORD

Sean Stephenson is one of those people whom you meet and never forget. He has an uncanny ability to motivate and inspire everyone he encounters. This young man exemplifies the power of belief and faith in yourself and your dreams. Sean believes in stretching himself to the limits of human potential. He is definitely a role model for anyone wishing to improve himself or herself.

I first met Sean at a time when I was feeling a lack of abundance in my life. Sean challenged me to look deep within myself and examine my limiting beliefs about money and my own self-worth. I took his advice to heart. Within a year, I married the man of my dreams and began working for myself, doing what I love best — writing and presenting fitness material to other people.

Just recently, I co-hosted a workout video with Sean to encourage people with and without physical disabilities to make exercise an important priority in life. Thanks to Sean's advice and my own dedication to improvement, I no longer lack abundance of any kind.

To this day, I carry a picture of Sean in my day planner to remind me to keep pushing forward, trying to do the things that I believed I could not do. I often use Sean's story to inspire others. I only wish that I had had access to Sean's book when I was a teenager!

– Ms. Fitness Universe, Kary Odiatu
See Kary online: www.fitlove.com
Also read her testimonial at the back of this book

AUTHOR'S NOTE

Dear Reader,

People often ask me why I wrote this book. I am sure, if I thought about it long and hard, I could come up with thousands of reasons. But the two main reasons that pop into my head are, "to share with teens and young adults that success is internal, not external" and "to spread the message that most human suffering is completely unnecessary."

Who am I to write about success, overcoming obstacles, confidence, and unnecessary suffering? Good question! Let's just start by saying I am not your ordinary young adult. On May 5, 1979, I entered this world fighting to survive. The doctors told my parents that I wouldn't even live past the first night. I was born with a rare bone disorder called Osteogenesis Imperfecta. This condition causes the bones to be stunted in growth and extremely brittle. Because of the disorder, I have had over 200 bone fractures and have to use a wheelchair to get around. In my life backpack, I also carry the challenge of being three feet tall. With all of my experiences, you can imagine how I can relate to obstacles and overcoming them to succeed.

For years, I would have traded my physical condition for anything until one day I realized that my physical challenge was a gift, not a burden. It was then that I acknowledged every individual as a living and breathing billboard. I decided that my billboard would convey a motivational and inspirational message to all those around me. I stopped dwelling on what I didn't have and began focusing on what I did have, which was the ability to inspire, energize, and educate audiences ranging from kindergarten classes to Congress. By the time I was eighteen years old I had addressed thousands of kids, teenagers, and young adults on topics such as substance abuse, self-confidence, and success. The most interesting thing that I have learned from speaking to youth is that, no matter what they look like or what their backgrounds are, they all enjoy succeeding and feeling good. Unfortunately, many kids don't know how to combine the two to create the ultimate life they deserve. So that's why I decided to write this book. I wanted to bridge the gap between succeeding and feeling good.

I readily admit that our generation faces thousands of challenges such as violence, drugs, sexually-transmitted diseases, discrimination, poverty, and the list goes on and on. So, if you are skeptical of how today's youth can succeed when they are just trying to survive, then I recommend this book and its testimonials with all my heart. Some might categorize this book as "self-help" but I prefer "motivational manual." If this is your first motivational manual, then welcome. Let me warn you that this book is like a match. If you just read it and don't apply the information, your match will sit motionless and ineffective. However, if you absorb and apply the information, stories, and advice, your match will create a burning drive to succeed.

While writing this book, I took into consideration your busy lifestyles with school, clubs, sports, dating, jobs, family, and so forth, that is why I made it short and to the point. I know you are asked to read quite a bit while attending school but trust me the following pages can impact your life in ways you never dreamed of. There are a few things you may want to know before you begin.

• I encourage and strongly recommend that you write down any questions, ideas, and thoughts that come to mind in your favorite journal and or notebook. So make sure to keep a pen handy as you read.

• This book was not written for any particular "clique" or "crowd." Everyone can benefit from *How YOUth Can Succeed!*.

- After each chapter, there are short activities designed to increase your confidence and success. Trust me, this is not a lame workbook filled with cheesy energizers meant to waste your time. The activities were created to improve the quality of your destiny.

- At the end of the book, I have included exciting testimonials from individuals who were willing to share their personal recipes for success.

- This is not a book to be read only once. Refer to it, as if it were a road map for success. Unlike many books that are meant to be read once and then collect dust, this is a motivational manual. This manual is a great investment for your future so read, re-read, and re-read it again as many times as needed. Repetition is one of the most powerful forces of success.

Attitude is everything, so buckle up and expect the best. ENJOY!

Respectfully yours,

Sean C. Stephenson
LaGrange, IL

CHAPTER
I

VISUALIZE
YOUR VOYAGE!

One-year visualization

Visualize Your Voyage!

One-year visualization

Hello and welcome, my friend. I am so glad you decided to join me on this powerful voyage. Trust me, this voyage is not an imaginary fairy tale; it is a journey of human potential. I will be with you as we pass through the violent storms to bright blue skies of success.

**You are the captain of this journey;
I am merely a guide with the compass.**

This journey will be the best adventure you have ever experienced without having to leave your chair.

If you were looking forward to reading something extremely long and boring, written by someone three times your age who may not understand your needs, I am afraid you selected the wrong book. I am a young adult on a crusade to maximize others' potential by recycling their negative emotions into empowering beliefs. How? By simplifying the strategies to success. This book will be like most things in life; the more you put into it, the more you will get out of it.

I wrote this book in a way that includes you, the reader. Your thoughts are as much a part of this book as mine, so make sure and write them down in a journal. You never know, maybe you'll get an idea for an Academy Award-winning movie, a best-selling book, or a solution to ending world hunger. You think that sounds too impossible to accomplish for someone your age? Well, stranger things have happened.

Take Craig Kielburger, for example. At just the age of twelve, he was so outraged after viewing a news story on child labor that he organized a nationwide organization called Free the Children. Now, as a young adult, he is responsible for one of the world's largest foundations committed to ending child labor. Who knows what amazing influence you may have on the world, so grab a pen as we depart on our voyage to unleashing the power of your human potential.

Have you ever heard this phrase?

"Sometimes we don't choose the books we read, they choose us."

Sound too crazy and mystical to be true? OK then, how did this book come into your life? Did you see it on a shelf in a bookstore, did a parent give it to you, or did you get it after one of my seminars? Why does this matter and how does it relate to success? Actually, it has more to do with success then you and I can ever imagine.

Success appears in our lives in similar fashion to the books we read. On the surface, it may appear that this book came into your life by accident; however, the true forces are deeper than that. This book appeared in your life as a direct result of two powers. Before I explain the two powers, I have an important question to ask you. Is life predetermined for everyone or do our decisions shape the outcomes of our future? Philosophers have been debating this question for centuries. What they have found is, in order to answer such an enormous question you have to view life either through the windows of *fate* or *destiny*. Those who believe in fate would say, "our situations are predetermined by a force outside of our control." People who believe in destiny would say, "situations in life are created by our decisions." I dare to believe in a combination of the two.

Every decision we make determines the future of our individual destiny. When everyone's destinies interact with each other, fate occurs. What happens to you in life is both a direct result of destiny and fate.

Therefore, this book appeared in your life as a direct result of destiny (your decisions) and fate (other people's decisions, such as mine to write this book). The beauty of this organized principle is, once you recognize that these two powers exist and that they shape your life, you will begin to succeed by adapting to them instead of chasing your tail in resistance.

So how do you adapt? That depends on the individual and what strategies they feel most comfortable using. What I can tell you for sure is, the use of strategies is the main ingredient to adapting. Lucky for you this entire book is filled with these strategies. Some of these strategies are extremely powerful and should not be used while operating heavy machinery.

Would you be interested in learning *right now* one of the most powerful strategies? However, if your life becomes extremely amazing and overloaded with success, don't say I didn't warn you. The powerful strategy I am about to explain has caused some of the most incredible moments in history. Unfortunately, most people overlook this powerful strategy because it is viewed as "obvious." *An important note*: Geniuses study, apply, and master the world's most obvious strategies. If, at any moment you feel uncomfortable studying the obvious, remind yourself that geniuses study the obvious — and you are a genius! This strategy is known as *visualization*.

I know what you might be thinking, "Sean I know how to visualize, what's the big deal?" Visualizing is more than just picturing something in your mind. Think about weightlifting. Most people know about it, right? However, does everyone lift weights? No. And, of the number of those who do lift weights, how many take it to the max, sculpting an amazing body? As you know, the answer is very few. The same principle holds true for visualization.

Everyone has the potential to use visualization to succeed but not everyone acts on this potential.

Why? Because most people never realize the power in properly using visualization. The good news I will share with you is how to properly use visualization as a strategy to succeed. In fact, once you learn this strategy, you will enhance your enjoyment of this book along with the quality of your destiny. Sound like something you would be interested in learning? Good! Here we go!

I have found there are two types of visualizations, observational and role-playing. If it helps you, think of them as two views in a video game. Role-playing is a first person perspective, meaning you view the world through the eyes of the character. The other, observational, is a bystander perspective, meaning you are not the character, you are only observing the character from a distance. When most people think of visualizing they picture themselves from an observational perspective. Let's do that now.

— Read the following activity, then close your eyes and do it. —

Picture in your mind that you are observing from a distance (as if you were a *Peeping Tom*) yourself at the end of a romantic date. It doesn't matter if you have been on one or not, we are merely visualizing. See yourself smiling while holding hands with your date. Notice how you lean forward to signal a sweet kiss goodnight. After agreeing with your body language, your date consents to a kiss by gently wrapping his/her fingers around the back of your neck to pull you in close. Then it happens, your lips meet and, *bang*, the visualization is over!

. . . .
Begin visualizing
. . . .

Did you do the assignment? If you answered yes (as I am sure you have), then you are more motivated than most individuals in society. If not, please do it right *now* because it is an important step in grasping the most powerful step of visualizing.

If you did visualize the previous assignment, how hard was it for you to see yourself outside your body? How did it make you feel watching yourself in this situation? How vivid did you make the visualization? Was it in color or black and white? Did it appear similar to a movie or a choppy slide show (several spaced images in time)? Was there sound? If you can't remember, that's OK just do it again and see what it looked like.

OK, now that you have experienced an observational visualization, let's crank our intensity up a notch. We'll transform our visualization from observational to role-playing. Personally when I make this transformation I like to say, "Batten down the hatches baby, I'm going in!" Instead of viewing it from an observational perspective this time we are going to visualize the scene through your eyes.

— Now read the following activity, then close your eyes and do it. —

Picture in your mind that you are standing at the front steps of your date's residence. You have just finished an excellent evening of dinner and a movie. Your body feels extremely tired because you were out late the night before. Your heart begins to race as you realize it is that time in the date when you need to send out a signal that you are interested in a kiss. Your heart beats almost out of your chest. As you hold your date's warm hands, your palms begin to sweat. Each breath is harder to inhale as if there were a load of bricks on your chest. To hide your fear, you place a giant smile on your face as you gaze deeply into your date's eyes. You slowly lean forward hoping your date will get a clue from your body language that you want a kiss. As you bend forward, your date lets go of your hands. Quietly his/her fingers rush up the back of your neck and begin to pull you in. Then it happens, your lips meet and, *bang,* the visualization is over!

. . . .

Begin visualizing

. . . .

So how did that feel? If you played "full-out" and really stepped into the visualization, I am sure it was much more intense, exciting, and empowering than your observational visualization. This is the visualization that I use the most to adapt to the powers of both fate and destiny. Role-playing visualizations create a stronger foundation of believability for your subconscious. The beauty behind this type of visualization is your brain becomes confused between what you have really experienced and what you have only visualized. Unlike most types of confusion, this creates positive opportunities. If your brain thinks you have previously done something, it will be more at ease doing it a second time even though the first time might have only been a vivid (role-playing) visualization.

Here is an example of what happens when I apply role-playing visualization to my life. As I mentioned earlier, I was born with a rare bone condition called Osteogenesis Imperfecta which stunts the growth of my bones, causing them to be extremely fragile. Picture that something as simple as sneezing has fractured my collarbone. Initially, when I break a bone it is extremely painful, although you would imagine I would get used to the pain considering the many bones broken in my lifetime. Unfortunately, each break is as painful, intense, and real as the last one.

During the few weeks and sometimes months that my bones are mending, I use role-playing visualization to accelerate the healing. I do this by lying down, closing my eyes, and remaining extremely still. I clear all of my thoughts and envision myself healing rapidly. I picture the bone growing back together even stronger and visualize the pain disappearing. Often I transition from role-playing to observational.

While in an observational visualization, I picture myself going through the several weeks of recovery. I speed up my visualization as if it were VCR tape on fast forward. I then return the visualization to normal speed and view my life four months into the future. I see myself pain free, happy, and extremely active again. I seize these images from the visualization and embed them deep into my conscious. Of course, when I open my eyes I am not instantly healed, but I am extremely confident that my recovery will be shorter and not as frustrating. Why? Because my brain has now been wired with positive images of what's to come.

Can you think of an experience or a time in your life when you could apply visualization? If you were positive that visualization would improve and enhance your future, would you definitely use it? Well it can and it will if you commit yourself to using it on a daily basis. Think of a group of people who would benefit from visualization. How about athletes on a sports team, how might they use this strategy? If the players create a strong visualization before walking onto the court that they will defeat their opponents no matter what, then what might occur? Their bodies would probably snap into a state of certainty, creating all the moves needed to be an unstoppable competitor in a game. I know visualizations alone can't win a game but let me ask you this, how would your chances of winning be if you entered a game with the mindset that you were going to be defeated? Slim to none, because what you visualize you begin to believe. And what you believe you begin to achieve.

What if I said, "I am very proud that you read this entire book"? Sure, that may sound weird considering that you have not even finished the first chapter. However, visualize (either by role-playing or observational means) that you just finished reading this book and now you are pumped full of incredible ideas and strategies to succeed.

For several months, on a daily basis, you begin referring to the book's information and testimonials plus the personal comments you made in your journal. After reading *How YOUth Can Succeed!*, you are now undergoing amazing emotional changes. The feelings of happiness and insight rush through your brain several times a day, causing you to be extremely intellectual. You begin attracting the love interest you have always wanted. Your grade report indicates that your scores are higher than they have ever been before. All of the projects that you used to be afraid of doing have now become simple and enjoyable.

Good! Now four years have passed and your life is filled with success way beyond your wildest dreams — all because of what you learned in this book.

See why I congratulated you in advance? If you comprehend the powers of this short book and how great life can be if you finish it, your mindset will be focused and determined to achieve all its great rewards. Most people who buy books never even finish them. I am sure there is a strong correlation between this fact and why most people never feel fulfilled in life. They give up mining seconds before they find the gold. That's what makes visualization so powerful. If you visualize all the rewards that come after finishing either a large or small project, your brain will remind you, "hey, I want those rewards so let's finish!" The stronger your visualization, the faster you can attain your goal. As you read this book, I will ask you to visualize moments in your past, present, and even future. I must remind you that, if you take the power of visualization and believe in it, this book will take your life to the next level. So I warn you to respect its amazing power and use it for only positive purposes. Just like fire, it will keep you warm in the cold months of your voyage but it will also burn you alive if you are careless with it.

Activity #1

• • • • • • • • • • •

Creating a strong foundation for your *one-year visualization*!

I want you to sit down alone somewhere and create a vivid observational visualization of yourself exactly one year from today. Visualize what positive improvements you want to make in your life. Picture how you will carry yourself, as you walk or wheel, with your newfound confidence. How do you want to act around those you are attracted to? What type of physical shape do you want to be in? Then, after a few minutes of observing as an outsider, step into yourself through a role-playing visualization.

How strong will you be? What, if any, physical pain will you eliminate from your body? How focused do you want your concentration skills to be? How will confidence appear in your tone of voice and vocabulary selection? How does it feel inhaling with gratitude and exhaling with a positive attitude? What type of attitude have you always wanted?

Now is the best time to visualize yourself with this attitude. Have fun and really give this visualization your all. Think of all the amazing experiences you can attract with this activity.

. . . .
Begin visualizing who you want to be exactly a year from NOW
. . . .

CHAPTER
II

THE
LIFE TRIAD

Thoughts ➤ *Words* ➤ *Actions*

The Life Triad

Thoughts ➤ *Words* ➤ *Actions*

I hope you enjoyed your visualization activity. If you made it this far, you are doing great! Now that you know the most powerful strategy for success, are you interested in learning other strategies and how they all interconnect to create unstoppable success?

OK, think of visualization as one unit, similar to a Lego block. Growing up, I built all kinds of things with Legos so I know that only one Lego block won't make anything. However, if you interlock one to a set of others, the possibilities of what can be built are endless. The more units (strategies) you have, the greater you can adapt, enjoy, and improve the situations in your life.

When I started studying human behavior a few years ago I realized that even though we all look different, come from different backgrounds, and have different lifestyles, we all follow similar behavioral patterns. Why? It is a phenomenon that exists because of the relationship between our egos and emotions. How would you like to learn one of the most powerful patterns of human behavior? It dictates how people react to their environment and circumstances. Once you fully comprehend this pattern, you can devise an approach to transform your one-year vision into reality. Enough talk, let's dive headfirst into discussing and applying this pattern.

In any situation, in our lives we revert to the pattern that I call The Life Triad. As you know, the prefix "tri" stands for three. Therefore there are three parts to this pattern: our thoughts, our words, and our actions. I like to think of them as three individual shapes. Picture our thoughts as a square, our words as a circle inside the square, and our actions as a triangle inside the circle.

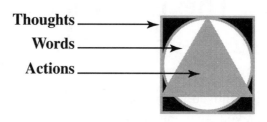

Here is how they inter-relate and develop into a powerful pattern of human behavior. What we think (our thoughts) transfers into what we say (our words). What we say transfers into what we do (our actions).

Is that too much info at once? Let's break it down into smaller bites of information starting with our thoughts.

THOUGHTS

Everything created by women and men originated from a thought. From the book you are reading, to the shoes you are wearing, to the bed you sleep on at night, they all began with a thought. Thoughts are the invisible catalysts behind all human inventions. Thoughts impact more than physically-constructed inventions such as books, shoes, and beds. Thoughts are the seeds of human emotion. If you only focus your thoughts on what you don't have, you most likely will live in a world of jealousy, frustration, and anger. If your thoughts are focused on helping people, you most likely will live in a world of philanthropy, contribution, and compassion.

Here is a question to ponder. Have you ever been angry? If not, then you must be super-human and I wish you well. However, the truth is most people at one time in their existence have experienced the emotion of anger. Emotions however are merely the growth of our thoughts. When people are sad it is not because sadness enters the body mysteriously. Sadness is the result of focusing on sad thoughts. The same holds true for anger. Next time you are angry, focus on nothing but loving, happy, and generous thoughts. I admit that holding a pleasant thought while angry is extremely difficult. But if done with commitment you will collapse your anger and reach inner harmony.

Don't get me wrong, I am not saying that everyone should be happy 100% of the time. I am merely saying that, if you have a destructive thought, such as anger or jealousy, simply be mindful that it has entered into your conscious. Then ask yourself these questions, "Do I want to continue holding on to this thought?" followed by, "What good will holding on to this thought serve?" If you are honest with yourself, you will realize that your destructive thoughts are not serving or improving your life or the lives of others. How honest you want to be with yourself will depend on how you answer those questions.

OK, great, how does this relate to the most powerful pattern of human behavior? Thinking is the first stage in the creation of our behavior. What you think about trickles down into every aspect of your life. What thinking affects most is how you feel. People ask me all the time how I can be so energetic, happy, and motivated even though I am "handicapped." My response is, "My physical condition does not own or define me. My level of energy and happiness is a conscious decision I make by focusing on constructive and exciting thoughts." I have to refrain from laughing when they respond, "Wow, Sean, that's wonderful. Unfortunately I am just not a positive person, I guess I am just a cynical kind of guy/gal." When a person says this they are choosing to believe that how they feel is uncontrollable. Rather, how you feel is the direct result of the thoughts you choose to hold.

Your thoughts are either a key to unlock the door to a world of happiness or a shovel to bury you in a grave of loneliness, the beauty is, the choice is yours.

Until you choose to be the *master* of your thoughts, you will remain a *servant* to them. Can you think of a time in your life when a single thought haunted or helped you? What did you do with this thought? Did you eventually succumb to its power or did you rise above it?

There are several times in my life that a single thought has carried me to victory. When I was selected to testify in front of the United States Senate Judiciary Committee in July of 1998, I was delighted and grateful to receive such a prestigious honor. When the day for my testimony finally arrived, I was ecstatic. I was going to be broadcast live on TV across the nation, that is something that will get your thoughts stirred up. All that morning I had a giant smile on my face that I am sure made me look extremely silly. I did my best to contain my extreme excitement, but it was tough. At least a hundred thoughts bounced around in my head, like "What if I mess up when speaking?"; "What are you going to say when you meet Senators Orrin Hatch and Strom Thurmond?"; and "What if you start sneezing and can't stop?"

For a short period of time I let my thoughts take charge of me instead of me taking charge of my thoughts. Once I realized this I grabbed hold of one driving thought, "Sean, you will be the best speaker that the United States Senate has ever heard!"

Sound a little silly? Well, this driving thought worked like a charm. As I rode from the hotel to Capitol Hill, I kept repeating it over and over, each time with more and more confidence. After two hours or so of waiting in the Senate Judiciary Chamber, it was my turn to speak. The words flowed smoothly out of my mouth with true sincerity and strong confidence. As I read my testimonial, I continued to hear a faint voice in the back of my head, "Keep it up, Sean, you are the best speaker the Senate has ever heard."

It was like my mind and body were on autopilot and all I had to do was continue repeating my driving thought. The only time I goofed up was when I realized how well I was doing. I thought, "This is easy, I don't need to continue repeating my driving thought." As soon as I let go of my driving thought, I jumbled up two words in my testimonial, which became extremely obvious. I immediately reverted back to my driving thought and finished my testimonial jumble-free. Are you beginning to see how some of the most obvious things we think about can impact what we say? This is because our thoughts trickle down from invisible concepts in our head to verbal communication, allowing our thoughts to appear in what we say. Now let's look at the importance of what we say.

WORDS

Have you ever heard the phrase, "talk is cheap?" I disagree, what we say is priceless.

In your life, if you think one thing and say another, the world only knows what you say.

This is why as a professional speaker I am very cautious about the words I use with my audience. If you are thinking, "OK, Sean, you're a speaker and words are important to you, but I like to blurt out words without any thought. I don't see what's the big deal."

You're right, it's not a big deal, — it is a GIANT DEAL! Words are extremely powerful because they are the external billboards of your thoughts and emotions. No one can read your mind, the only way to know what you are thinking is to examine your words. If you only use destructive words, what message are you sending to others? Yep, you guessed it…that you only have destructive thoughts. As unfair as this may be, I call this phenomena **T-POV: The Power of Vocabulary.** The words and phrases you use consistently in your personal vocabulary illustrate your thoughts and emotions to the world. Whether you think that is or isn't true in your case doesn't matter, unfortunately. You may only have positive thoughts, but, if all you do is complain or use destructive language, that is all the world knows of you.

T-POV influences more than just those around you, it influences you. Whatever you say out loud is stored in your brain as something important to remember. This is why saying something like, "I am a loser" is extremely dangerous. Even though it may appear that verbalizing that comment is not that big of a deal, trust me, *it is.* When you verbalize a negative thought, it is remembered and stored in your subconscious. If you say, "I am a loser" your subconscious hears this and stores it. Because your conscious mind wants to please you, it will act on what is stored in your subconscious. The good news is whatever positive thoughts you verbalize will be stored and remembered the same way. This is why I constantly verbalize my positive thoughts.

I talk to myself all the time. I tell myself, "Sean you are doing great, I am so proud of you." Now that might sound crazy, but it works. The more you convince yourself that you are doing well, the more you will continue to improve. With everything that is going on in your life you NEED to be your own friend, coach, and student if you want to succeed. To be all three of these people, I recommend visualizing and verbalizing constantly.

The Power of Vocabulary is in the words we use in our everyday dialogues. Our vocabulary and the metaphors we use determine how we view reality. For instance, what one word would you use to describe life? Surprisingly, everyone has their own words to define life. Here are a few sample responses: "life is a game," "life is a blessing," "life is a struggle." If one word can mean all the difference in how you view the world, imagine what impact your entire vocabulary has. What may seem to be an insignificant detail such as correcting your vocabulary can often be the determining factor of whether success arrives at your door or skips your house entirely.

How many times do you use the destructive term, "Man, this _____ is killing me!" What type of message does that send to your brain? Do you think it leaves a constructive or destructive foundation for your life? If you said destructive, you're 100% correct. Please note that I am merely emphasizing the importance of what you say and how it affects you long term. Take these two phrases, for example. "School is killing me" and "School is challenging me." When you attach serious words to your emotions such as "this is killing me," you can be sure your outlook for success will diminish. However, there is as much importance in using empowering words as there is in avoiding destructive words.

Let's take an example from your life. Do you talk to yourself? Most people are afraid of talking to themselves. This is because in our society we have created a stigma against self-dialogue. If you told people that you talk to yourself, they might think you were loony. However, the power of self-dialogue (talking to yourself) is one of the best-kept secrets of success. Remember my earlier comment that your conscious connects your voice to your subconscious? The more you repeat constructive, positive, and motivating comments out loud, the more you wire your brain to succeed.

Here is an example from my life when I used **The Power of Vocabulary** to wire my brain. I was a disc jockey for our school's radio station when I was a freshman in high school. All DJs had to be licensed by the Federal Communication Commission if they were going to be on the air. To be licensed, you had to pass a complicated standardized test. You know, one of those kinds of tests that require a number two pencil. It was a good thing I wired my brain with **The Power of Vocabulary** before I went in to take that test.

I repeated to myself, "Sean, you can do this!" Had I not said this, I might not have pushed myself when things got rough. Most did not pass it the first time. I admit it took me seven times to pass that test. The only thing that drove me not to give up was my vocabulary. I kept repeating, "Sean you can do this!" My brain was so wired to believe my vocabulary I knew I couldn't leave until I passed. Who knows what might have been the outcome if I'd said, "Sean, give up, you already failed the test six times."

At the time I had no clue but now, after studying human behavior for the past few years, I realize that it was **The Power of Vocabulary** that carried me through to victory. Can you think of a time in your life when **The Power of Vocabulary** helped you through an exciting or frustrating time? What were the exact words you used? If you can't think of a time when **The Power of Vocabulary** assisted you, that's OK. Think of how you can use **The Power of Vocabulary** to carry yourself to victory.

So now that we have covered the importance of our thoughts and our words, let's look at the importance of our actions.

ACTIONS

When a person thinks about something and then shares it aloud with themselves or with others they are heading towards action. Our actions are the third and final piece to the puzzle of human behavior. What we do is the final product in the Life Triad. The phenomenon known as "road rage" is a good example of the combination of thoughts, words, and actions. Road rage is the term used to describe the behavior of people who allow their tempers to escalate while driving. Maybe you have been a victim or a culprit of road rage. If so, then this will sound very familiar.

Visualize yourself driving on an expressway. There is absolutely no traffic and you are sailing along comfortably at 55 miles an hour, when all of a sudden a semi-truck passes you on the left. Then it quickly cuts you off, missing your front bumper by three feet. At this point, what thoughts and emotions are running through your head? Are you scared, furious, or both? Surprisingly, what you think now will heavily determine the outcome of your life.

If you think, "this guy is going to pay" then what will happen? Your thoughts will transfer into words. I have noticed that, even if a driver is alone, sometimes he or she voices aggressive thoughts. When you do this, you are signaling to your brain that this is an important enough matter to be verbalized. So you blurt out, "I can't believe this jerk, he needs to be taught a lesson." Remember what your words transfer into? If you said actions, you are correct. So you slam on your accelerator and ride the truck's back bumper. Then, out of nowhere, the truck slams on its brakes. You end up dead with a face full of steel at fifty-five miles per hour. Had you just stopped yourself in the thought stage, without reinforcing it in the word stage, you might still be alive. I am sure you could think of thousands of examples where action in the Life Triad applies. I used road rage because almost everyone who drives has experienced it or been riding with someone who has. Can you think of an example when your thoughts transferred into words, and your words transferred into actions?

It is important to know that The Life Triad is not always 100% effective. Sometimes you may think about getting an "A" on a test. You then tell yourself out loud that you are going to get an "A." You then study extremely hard and do your very best on the exam. However, what happens if you get the score back and you only got a "B?" First, look back at the triad and see what could be improved. Maybe you need a stronger driving thought or saying. Maybe you need to improve your actions, how you studied. What really matters above everything else is that you were conscious of the pattern every step of the way. Had you not shot for an "A" you might have gotten a "C" or "D." The more you strengthen the areas of your triad, the more you will strengthen your success.

Activity #2
• • • • • • • • • • •

Using the life triad in your own life!

Although it may appear that this activity will not take long, give it some thought and seriously use what you create. Don't rob yourself of all of the amazing experiences you can attract with this activity.

– Thoughts –

Create a single thought that will drive you to become the person you imagined in your visualization in **Activity #1**.

For instance, "I can and will step into the
healthy body I deserve!"

(Write it down in your journal.)

— Words —

Great! Now create a single phrase that will drive
you to become the person you imagined in your
visualization in **Activity #1**.

For instance, "I can and will sculpt a healthy
and unstoppable body!"

(Write it down in your journal.)

— Actions —

Outstanding! Now create action that will allow you
to become the person you imagined in your
visualization in **Activity #1**.

For instance, "Today I will walk or jog two miles
and avoid eating between meals!"

(Write it down in your journal.)

CHAPTER
III

LENSES
OF BELIEF

*What you believe you can **achieve**!*

Lenses of Belief

What you believe you can <u>achieve</u>!

I hope you are enjoying your voyage so far. You have learned so much in such a short time and for that you should be extremely proud of yourself. Even if the book ended here, you would have many tools and strategies to succeed. Unfortunately, all the tools in the world won't help you if you don't believe in them or yourself, that's why I wrote this chapter. I want to help you develop your understanding of believing and how it can and will transform your dreams into reality. If you are committed to becoming the person in your *one-year visualization*, then you certainly need to have the power of believing on your side as we continue on our voyage.

Do you think a person's beliefs affect their individual reality? Do you think your beliefs affect your reality? If you said yes, you are right. I have found after studying human behavior that an individual's beliefs determine how he or she perceives reality. For example, if you believe that everyone is out to make a profit, how might you treat someone if they tried to help you? You would automatically assume that there was a catch and that their generosity had a hidden price tag. If you believed that all athletes were stupid, what might you think if the captain of your school's cheerleading or football team had a 4.0 GPA? You would probably jump to the conclusion that she or he cheated. Belief affects more than just how you view people in your reality, it also affects how you view yourself.

Think about a time in your life when you believed you weren't attractive or that no one would ever want to date you. I know when I was a sophomore in high school this belief surfaced in my life on many occasions. Guess what I did with this belief? Here is a hint, I transferred it into the second step of the Life Triad. You got it. I began verbalizing it to myself. The more I verbally focused on this belief, the more it became part of my reality. Whenever I met a girl, I automatically assumed she thought I was only cute. Not, "Oh he is so sexy, I want to kiss him *right now!*" kind of cute. More like, "Aww he reminds me of my little brother" kind of cute. Anyway, how do you think I felt about myself when I was holding this belief? If you said anything similar to "lousy," you are right on the money. How can belief have so much power over someone? This is because when a person believes in something with enough passion, their belief actually becomes a part of their reality, even though it may not truly exist. Here is a quick story demonstrating my point.

A group of rabbits was traveling through a field when, all of a sudden, two of them fell into a deep pit. All the other rabbits gathered around the pit to see what happened. They saw that the two rabbits were stuck standing on a thin ledge. After observing their struggle for some time they yelled, "Give up, you will never get out of there." The two rabbits ignored their cynical comments and continued to attempt to jump up out of the pit. The other rabbits kept yelling to them, "Give up, you are as good as dead." Finally, one of the rabbits took their advice. He simply gave up by falling off the ledge, falling to his death at the bottom of the pit. Yet the other rabbit continued to jump as high as he could. As the crowd of cynical rabbits yelled, "Give up and put yourself out of your misery," he began jumping even higher. Finally this rabbit made it out. The other rabbits asked him, "Why did you continue jumping? Didn't you hear us tell you to give up?" The rabbit explained to them that he was deaf and that he thought they were encouraging him the whole time not to give up.

How did what the two rabbits believe determine their realities? One rabbit believed that he couldn't make it out of the pit so, in his reality, the only way to end his frustration was death. This destructive type of belief is known as a limiting belief because it dismantles your outlook on the future. The other rabbit, who was deaf, believed that he could make it out alive because in his reality he was receiving encouragement from the other rabbits. His constructive type of belief is known as an empowering belief because it builds confidence for the future. This concept applies to more than just fictitious rabbits.

Eating disorders involving teenage girls and sometimes boys are an example of beliefs affecting reality. When someone with this disorder looks in the mirror, they often see an overweight person even though in reality they may be dangerously thin. Why is this? Well I am not a doctor or a therapist but I can tell you my conclusion from people I have known with eating disorders. When a person with an eating disorder looks in the mirror, he or she actually believes someone overweight is reflected there. How is this possible? I found the answer to that question a few months ago when I accidentally transposed the phrase, "seeing is believing." I read the phrase as, "believing is seeing." At that very moment, my whole outlook on believing changed. When I thought about my simple reading error, I realized, that what a person sees in life is filtered by their lenses of belief. So, until someone with an eating disorder changes his or her lens of belief, only an overweight person will be reflected in the mirror.

Do you now accept that the power of belief can actually destroy someone? Can you imagine if belief has the power to destroy someone what it can do for someone who harnesses its power for good? What you believe can also be used to create unstoppable success. This is why, as an inspirational speaker, I include for my audience activities, stories, and/or personal examples from my life that emphasize the power believing has in creating success.

I first realized this a few years ago when I read the quote, **"what you believe you can achieve."** Those six words, from a book full of quotes, suddenly jumped off the page and into my soul. I sat holding the book frozen like a deer caught in the headlights of a semi-truck barreling towards it. Prior to this time, I had read hundreds of similar quotes but none of them shook me like this one. I was actually frozen in what I call "thoughts of possibility." My mind imagined all the things I wanted to accomplish but thought would never happen because I was just an average guy. I was so thrilled that I could not stop squirming around in my wheelchair. I wanted to climb on the table and scream, "Hey, everyone, did you know what you believe you can achieve?" And no, I was not under the influence of drugs or alcohol.

I know there are hundreds of quotes, phrases, and stories that emphasize the power belief has in success. Just think of all the stories that you read as a kid like "The Little Engine That Could." However, just because you and I are aware of these stories doesn't mean that we necessarily believed in them. My question to you is;

What would your life be like right now if you stopped just listening to powerful messages and started believing them?

For instance, where would you be if you really believed that "the world is your playground?" Would you be afraid of things or would you run around carefree enjoying every moment?

Where would you be if you believed "do unto others as you would have them do unto you"? Would you treat everyone with hate and ignorance or with love and understanding? Our lives can be so incredible if we start believing powerful advice.

I know I am glad I started believing "what you believe you can achieve." This viewpoint encouraged me never to give up, even when I questioned my capabilities while preparing this book. Without the power of belief, I would have stopped writing the first time a challenge arrived in the early stages. This book is in your hands right now because, whenever a limiting belief entered into my conscious, I acknowledged it and then canceled it out with hundreds of empowering beliefs.

I won't lie, at times I did question my capabilities. *Have you* ever questioned your own capabilities? If you have you are not alone, almost everyone does. But what separates those who achieve their goals from those who don't is simple. Those who never encourage themselves when they begin to question their own talent and knowledge often give up. However, those who question themselves and immediately follow up their questioning with an empowering belief such as, "my capabilities are virtually unlimited because *what I believe I can achieve!*", are the ones who triumph. Take my word for it, after traveling around the world, working with everyone from kindergartners to the President of the United States, I have found that

every individual, including yourself, has the potential to achieve all that is believed.

This is because

your personal capabilities are only as strong or as weak as your lenses of belief.

What you believe determines whether you will succeed or not.

Just look at some of the legends in American history, Abraham Lincoln, Thomas Edison, and Rosa Parks. What do you think they all had in common? The answer is they all believed in something i.e., democracy, electricity, and equality. So what separates them from anyone else? They are remembered because they believed in something with enough passion that their beliefs alone carried them through the three stages of the Life Triad. And, boy, I am glad they did because I would not want to imagine the world today had these three individuals not stepped *up* for what they believed in.

Belief affects every outcome from the course of history to the actions you take in your life. When I ponder that statement, I immediately think about my close friend, Kary Odiatu. Kary competes in international fitness competitions. In 1998, she placed third in the Ms. Fitness Olympia contest in Greece. A few months later she went on to win the highest title of Ms. Fitness Universe in Las Vegas, Nevada. I asked her how she beat the two competitors that placed above her early that year in the Ms. Fitness Olympia contest. She writes in her testimonial:

"I worked hard on my routine and used the third-place finish in Greece and my desire to better it as motivation to push through the physical exhaustion that I was feeling from all of the traveling and training. I knew that I had to be better than I ever had been before. I focused all my attention on being a winner and doing the best job possible."

In essence, her belief drove her to victory. Success twinkled in her eyes and rushed through her veins when she took charge of her destiny by believing in herself.

Belief can have that same impact on you. There are so many challenges facing youth right now that this concept is certainly difficult, but not impossible, to accept. No one lives his or her life from start to finish without problems and challenges. I am sure at times your life has been harsh, confusing, and frustrating. Being a teenager and a young adult is a process of sorting empowering beliefs from limiting beliefs. Just like my friend, Kary, what you believe in life you tend to attract, accomplish, and or become. If you are convinced that your limiting beliefs are true, you will only attract a destructive future. What if you had a limiting belief that you were a loser? You would actually become one simply because you believe it. "What, that's not very motivational." You're right, it's not motivational, but it is true. Your mind is more advanced than you and I can imagine. It is also very protective, and it doesn't like disappointing you. So if you tell it you are a loser, it will begin to act like one. It does this in order to satisfy your demands. If you believe you will never make the honor role in school, score a date with the person you like, or be picked for the team, you are absolutely correct. However if you tell yourself:

you are a conscientious student, an attractive individual, or an outstanding athlete, your mind will fuel the fires of your intelligence, confidence, and or physical strength.

You will begin to live out the qualities of whatever empowering beliefs you create.

If you believe deep inside that you are capable of being an outstanding athlete, actor, singer, dancer, artist, movie producer, or whatever your interest is, then you can make it happen.

Here is an example from my life when an empowering belief built a strong foundation for success. Remember I mentioned that when I was in high school I was a radio disc jockey? Well, I was also a member of the school TV club. Our school was fortunate enough to have its own cable television station that broadcast to all of the suburbs nearby. As a freshman, I hosted an interview program called "Small Talk" but I only produced two episodes. During the end of the year I thought to myself, "Sean, no one is really interested in your talk show because the concept has been done before by other students. What you need is a program that is original and creative and involves more students then just yourself." So I decided to produce a teen saga called, "Living Through High School." It involved a cast and crew of 22 high school students.

People told me it couldn't be done. Even the faculty advisor told me it was "wishful thinking" to tackle such a monster of a production. In order to avoid the cynics, I created a strong empowering belief to cancel them out. On several occasions I reminded myself that

throughout history people who said, "It can't be done!" or "That is impossible!" were interrupted by others who said, "We just did it."

I didn't care what anyone else said, I had faith in my empowering beliefs and my creative skills. My empowering belief, that I could create a teen saga, finally paid off. Not only was the show voted the most-watched program on the station but it also won awards in a high school video festival. The program was loved so much that numerous Chicago area newspapers featured it as one of the most exciting and creative high school television programs ever. Yet the cynics said it couldn't be done. This is when I realized that cynics are just permanent residents in their houses of limiting beliefs. When Walt Disney first began his career, the cynics thought his ideas were silly and that they would never succeed. But he believed in his ideas to the point that he actually visualized Disneyland years before it was ever built.

When you believe with all of your empowering beliefs that you will thrive and survive, you will. It is important to remember that belief alone will only serve as the foundation to your achievements; you have to build the structure of success. Even though many people felt that my television show was successful, it still took thousands of hours to write, produce, and edit. That is why I stressed in the last chapter that all of the positive thoughts and words in the world are useless without taking action. Think of your empowering beliefs as the flashlight and your actions as the batteries.

Your empowering beliefs alone will only shine as bright as your actions.

Activity #3
• • • • • • • • • • • •

"Limiting beliefs will limit you."
"Empowering beliefs will empower you."

As you now know, what you believe you can achieve, but what if you believe things that are holding you back? These beliefs are called "limiting beliefs" because they are limiting your potential for success. For example:

- *"I have always been fat so I could never be thin."*

- *"I have always gotten bad grades so I can't get A's."*

- *"I am too young for anyone to take my business idea seriously."*

List three limiting beliefs in your life that have restricted you in the past from becoming the person you want to be in your *one-year visualization.*

(Write them down in your journal.)

The opposite of "limiting beliefs" is "empowering beliefs." These beliefs maximize your potential and can empower you to *achieve* success. On the next few lines, write down some empowering beliefs that will fuel your voyage of becoming the person in your *one-year visualization.*

For example:

- *"If I exercise and eat right, I will create the healthiest body!"*

- *"If I focus more on my studies, my grades will be OUTSTANDING!!!"*

- *"No one can hold me back from my dreams because youth is on my side!"*

List six empowering beliefs in your life that will jumpstart you to live as the person in your *one-year visualization.*

(Write them down in your journal.)

CHAPTER
IV

You Must

---

*In life, **you must** do the things
you think you cannot do!*

You Must

*In life, <u>you must</u> do the things you think
you cannot do!*

Was it easy for you in the last activity to list your empowering beliefs? Hopefully, yes. Whenever I ask people to list their empowering and limiting beliefs, they have an easier time listing all their limiting ones. Why is this? Limiting beliefs rationalize why people aren't living out their dreams. Sadly, people rationalize their whole life away and they do this in one word. Do you know what this one destructive, limiting, and enslaving word is?

It is "can't." Unfortunately, "can't" has become an acceptable pardon from attaining individual achievement. The word has become almost a permanent scapegoat for those afraid to grow and learn. When someone uses the term can't, they really mean: "I don't want to," "I am afraid," "I don't have to," "there is nothing in it for me," or "what if I fail?" Don't get me wrong, we've all had times when the word "can't" pops into our vocabulary. The important question is what did you do after you said "can't?" Did you believe it and give up or did you recycle its power and succeed? Whenever I use this term I stop and ask myself, "Sean, do you really mean that or is that an excuse you are hiding behind?" When I ask myself this question, it forces me to be honest with myself and realize that "can't" is nothing but an excuse.

So when was the last time you said "can't?" Did you say it to a friend, parent, or teacher? I hear people use the word all the time. Just recently a friend/college classmate of mine told me she "can't" get over a painful argument with her parents. I looked her straight in the eye and said, "and you never will." That blew her hair back. She immediately got defensive and told me that I was out of line for saying that. I told her;

"If you think you can or you think you can't — you're right!"

As long as my friend believes she "can't" get over her dispute, she will continue to carry her anger, frustration, and, most of all, pain, everywhere she goes.

Remember in Chapter Two when I mentioned T-POV (The Power of Vocabulary) and in Chapter Three when I mentioned the power of belief? If you mix the power of belief with the vocabulary word "can't," you now have a strong potion for misery and personal enslavement. Life is so amazing if you set yourself free from "can't." This is why I have dedicated my life to abolishing this word from people's vocabulary and mindset. I know I set myself free by believing that in life *you must* do the things you think you cannot do. I am not saying if you think you can't jump off a bridge, you should go out and do it. I am talking about going out and doing the things that would improve your life, or "positive risks." Here is an example from my life when I took a positive risk by doing something I thought I couldn't do.

When I was a junior in high school I participated in a program called American Legion Boys State. Boys and Girls State are week-long camps held in almost every state in the union. At these camps, juniors in high school learn the democratic process first-hand by running mock campaigns and elections for all the positions in state government.

My first day at Boys State I was very nervous. So I did what my instincts told me, "Do the things you think you cannot do." I went around and introduced myself to every guy I could. The friends I made there in one week were tighter then the ones I had made in school. A group of my new friends encouraged me to run for governor, the highest office at Boys State. I was the shortest guy and the only one in a wheelchair at Boys State, so I was a little hesitant. Only one person could be governor out of 1,000 individuals and truthfully, after just coming off a loss in high school for student council president, I wasn't quite sure if luck was on my side. However, that week I learned that success and victory have little to do with luck and more to do with vision and belief in yourself.

The night of the first round of speeches, I visualized myself receiving a standing ovation. I envisioned speaking with confidence and sincerity. I envisioned winning the primary and advancing to the next round, and that's exactly what I did. I wheeled up on stage and transformed myself into the greatest three-foot-tall leader the world has ever seen. All I did was turn my dreams into reality by following my vision. I received the standing ovation along with the nomination from the party, which advanced me into the final round.

I followed the same format when I addressed the entire Boys State audience. I spoke on stage as if I was talking directly to each of the 1,000 young men. My message must have made the right impact because I won the election with flying colors. To this day, I recall that week as the best one of my life. Not just because I came home with the title of governor, or because I made some of the most incredible friendships, it was because I came home believing that I could do the things that I thought I couldn't do before. Because of my new attitude, a series of events occurred in my life over the following four years that led me to where I am now, writing to you. Four years ago, when I ran for governor, I was unsure if I could win, however, I pushed myself to do what I thought I couldn't do and because of this a world of amazing possibilities has unfolded. People who take action on the things they think they cannot do are the ones who truly taste the juice of life.

Pushing yourself to do the things you think you cannot do applies to more than just large projects like running for an election. It also applies to daily activities. For instance, let's look at exercise. Have you ever been lifting weights for over an hour when you thought of stopping before finishing your last set of reps? But, for some reason, you found the energy and strength to push yourself to override your lazy thoughts and finish. How is this possible? This is because your mind took over and said to your body, "If we think we can't, then *we must!*" Your body and mind will only grow if you do the things you think you cannot do. Anyone who is extremely successful will tell you that major success does not come by doing the things you know you can do. If that were the case, we would all still be living in caves and working by the light of torches.

Do you think your favorite actor/actress, musician, or athlete reached their goals by doing only the little things they were sure they could do? Absolutely not! People who are well known like Michael Jordan or even the late Walt Disney brought their lives to another level because they took positive risks with their destiny. They broke out of their fears and into a level I call the *Kingdom of Success*. In this kingdom, people take action on their fears by doing the things they think they cannot do.

Follow me for a moment while I describe this *Kingdom of Success*. Imagine a giant castle built on top of an enormous white cloud. Below is a planet of people wandering around like zombies, going to work and school, all enslaved by the word "can't." However, in the *Kingdom of Success*, "can't" is immediately replaced with "can." If you are willing to set yourself free from can't, you may enter the *Kingdom of Success*. The voyage to this kingdom may appear difficult but it is free to anyone at any time.

My good friend and teacher, Jaime Alanis, is a great example of someone who entered the *Kingdom of Success*. When he was a kid he lived in a dangerous neighborhood in Chicago. Most of his friends and peers ended up either in prison or killed by drugs, violence, or gangs. He knew he could easily follow their path and end up in a life of misery but he wanted more from life. He knew that to succeed he had to do what he thought he couldn't do. As seen in the following excerpt from his testimonial:

*"When I started senior year, my mentor highly recommended that I attend graduate school. At first, I thought he was just trying to boost my ego. When he insisted that he would assist me in the process of applying, I knew he was serious. **I had great doubts about my chances** of getting accepted since my grade point average was not as high as the requirements stipulated. My mentor decided to intervene in the process and vouch for me. I was finally accepted on a probationary basis. I had to prove that I was up to the academic standards of graduate school. At this point, I was hungry for knowledge, I was devouring books and articles like there was no tomorrow. I wanted to know the secrets of the universe. It took me five years to complete a study on street gangs that served as my master's thesis. When I submitted it to the chair of the Department of Sociology, he asked me if I would be interested in teaching an introductory course in sociology. I now teach introduction to sociology to students and continue to work with and mentor youth in the Little Village community."*

Did you notice when Jaime made the transition into the *Kingdom of Success*? It took place when he took action on his doubts and entered graduate school even though he wasn't sure he would make it. Because he took this positive risk, he is now able to motivate and educate hundreds of students a year. Had he denied his mentor the offer of applying for graduate school because he thought he couldn't do it, he would have missed out on several opportunities. One of them would have been having me as a student, later giving him the chance to share his experiences with you.

You never know what wonderful opportunities await you if you were to take positive risks in your life such as staying in school, introducing yourself to someone you have always wanted to know, or learning a new skill. You may not have realized it but you are a taking a positive risk right *now* by reading this book. The greatest opportunities are waiting to occur if you are committed to acting on your ideas.

Activity #4
• • • • • • • • • • •

A visit to the destiny store!

OK! Visualize you are in a department store. This is not an ordinary store. It sells exciting things for your destiny. One aisle sells nothing but chances to meet anybody you want (i.e., Sandra Bullock, the Dalai Lama, or maybe one of your long-lost relatives). Another sells trips to anywhere you want to go in the world (i.e., London, Australia, or maybe Idaho). Another sells emotions and attitudes you have always wanted to have (i.e., patience, understanding, or confidence). And the last aisle sells opportunities and experiences you have never had (i.e., work for the President, compete in the Olympics, or star in a movie). In this Destiny Store you have just enough money to buy three things from each of the four aisles. Sounds silly but this is no joke. The most important part about doing things in life you thought you could never do is first deciding what you want.

Think of three people you would like to meet someday. Take your time and have some fun.

(Write them down in your journal.)

Great!!! Visualize three places you would like to visit if you could travel anywhere in the world.

(Write them down in your journal.)

Outstanding! How about three emotions you want to experience on a daily basis.

(Write them down in your journal.)

Brilliant! Really take your time and decide on what three things you would like to experience in your lifetime.

(Write them down in your journal.)

There are so many things to see and do in life that, once you know what you want to experience, you are one step closer to accomplishing the things you thought you couldn't do. In the following chapter, you will learn how to apply these experiences in a formula that will transform them from dreams into reality.

CHAPTER
V

FORMULA
FOR SUCCESS

Success is a dream with a plan!

Formula for Success

Success is a dream with a plan!

After years of working with several organizations and institutions, from the White House to a college university, I have formed my own opinion regarding success. The word *success* is used frequently today on TV, in movies, and on the Internet. There must be a thousand books alone written about how to succeed.

Why? We live in an age where there is a flood of information, resources, and things to do. However, this benefit has caused an epidemic of societal instability and lack of guidance, especially among those in our generation. Just look at the divorce, suicide, and substance abuse rates in America today. People are hungry for direction, supervision, and leadership, and they are reaching out to anything that will bring peace and certainty. Thus the dawn of the "self-help" age. It seems as if you can turn on television at any time, day or night, and find programs dedicated to helping people succeed either through God, family, community, exercise, or whatever. You may have even seen on TV late at night my good friend and mentor, Tony Robbins. He, like myself, promotes programs filled with strategies to create the life people deserve to live. And we are not alone in this industry. There are hundreds of personal development speakers and authors, all promoting the fundamental principles and universal themes of success. So why do people support such a field? I think it is only natural for people to want to succeed. I chose the word succeed as part of the book's title because I believe most of us would to like to succeed.

I believe you want to succeed because, if you didn't, you wouldn't have made it to this stage on our voyage. So, with that insight, I will unlock and reveal the magical formula for being successful. Follow this formula and you will succeed way beyond your wildest dreams. Are you ready? Maybe you should sit down for this. The formula for success is surprisingly simple. In fact, even a first-grader could understand it;

Success occurs when an individual combines their dreams with a plan and then takes action.

I am sorry, were you expecting a long boring explanation that involved long division or quantum physics?

Now I am sure in some of the thousand-page books on how to succeed there are probably two-hundred-page formulas dedicated to obtaining success. I am sure you don't mind that I have boiled it down into one sentence. I know it must sound too generalized. When I first started reading books about success, I thought to myself, "Well, easy for these authors to claim their strategies work, they are adults with an education, a career, and money." I thought that there was no way these authors could understand my life. I was fifteen to twenty years younger than they were, in a wheelchair, with zero personal cash flow. I "believed" that their strategies couldn't possibly apply to me. I said to myself, "Where do these yahoos get off telling me that if I apply their success models I could achieve all of my dreams?" But I am here to tell you that their strategies work. And so will mine, especially if you apply them immediately to your life.

I realize that in our culture we tend to point our fingers at fancy cars and big homes and say, "Man, the person who owns those must be successful." In actuality, success has very little to do with possessions and a lot to do with fulfillment and improvement. Money, cars, and homes are all nice to have but they do not equal success.

Not everyone one is successful. But anyone is capable of being a success. Just as anyone is capable of being nice or loving.

Success begins just like an emotion you might experience. First, you make the conscious decision to be and feel successful. The catch is you need to attach your emotions to an outcome, something you want. Dreams cannot be created without first deciding what you want out of life. If you are a person who experiences fear, anxiety, or lack of enthusiasm for making these decisions, I have some good and bad news for you. First, let's start with the bad news. Making decisions and creating dreams are to the mind what exercise is to the muscles. Your decision muscles may be extremely atrophied and will eventually cause you to miss out on the best moments of your life, producing enormous amounts of physical and or emotional pain. But there is still hope in the good news. It is not too late to exercise your decision muscles and return them to top Olympic strength. In the activity at the end of this chapter, I will give you a list of simple tasks in order to strengthen your decision muscles.

First, let's look at how this formula for success relates to projects of all sizes. Let's apply it to studying for an exam. If you visualize receiving an "A" on the exam, you are applying the dream portion of the equation. To strengthen the dream, you need to visualize all the wonderful results that could happen if you accomplished such a task. Such as how proud you would feel, how your teachers and parents would admire your dedication, and how this excellent grade would help build on your chances of a scholarship towards college. Once you have created a dream fixed in visualization, you are halfway there.

Now comes the portion of the equation people worry about the most — **the plan**. Take your dream of scoring an "A" on your test and apply it to a step-by-step plan of attack. Write out all the steps it will take you to score an "A." For instance, write out a detailed study schedule of when you will study, for how long, and what you will study (exact chapters, pages, and/or books). Then write out all of the resources you have, such as a parent, friend, or teacher who might help you understand the material better. What's the big deal with writing down all of your resources you ask? Extremely successful people in all fields follow this formula. When you write down all of your resources, you are building a bridge for your dreams to cross over into reality. After that, all you have to do is take action by crossing your bridge. It doesn't matter if you are a student or a business tycoon, once you have formulated a detailed plan and a solid dream, all you need to do is take action and believe in yourself.

Contrary to popular belief, success is not reserved just for certain people in this world. A person who loves shining shoes on a street corner for a living can be just as successful as a multi-billionaire who owns his/her own software company. This is because every day you take action on your dreams by following your plans you are a success. I am quite positive you have had several dreams throughout your life. Maybe you wanted to be an astronaut, a lawyer, or an opera singer. But how many plans have you created to make those dreams a reality? Almost everyone has dreams of doing something or being something. However, only those who create plans and act upon them are successful.

What is a dream (and not the kind you get when you fall asleep in class)?

A dream is just a collection of thoughts regarding your future.

We have thousands of thoughts a day. At birth we were all given one thing; an imagination. Granted, some imaginations are more vivid than others because they get more exercise, however, we are all capable of strengthening our imaginations with practice. Next time you are sitting as a passenger in a car, bus, or plane, with nothing to do, I want you to focus on what you want to accomplish. Close your eyes and visualize what all the details would look like as if you were really there floating above everything. Who is involved? What are people saying? What are you doing?

Then, after viewing the dream as a floating bystander, step into the role. Imagine you are talking to people and interacting with your environment. This strategy allows you to paint your dreams into your life masterpiece. When you begin to feel the excitement from the dream rush through your veins, open your eyes and take action. After doing this exercise, write down all the resources accessible to you that would transform your dream into a reality. If you play full out with this process, you will be quite surprised how you will begin to attract things from your dreams into your life.

Do you understand all that? If not, what are you going to do? Yep, re-read the previous paragraphs because there is no shame in reinforcement. I do it all the time and that is why I believe I am extremely successful.

So then, what's a plan you ask?

A plan is simply a roadmap, blueprint, and channel for your dreams to transform them into reality.

The best plans are written down for three reasons. The first is so you can call upon on them again at anytime in their original written state of intensity. The more specific your written plans, the shorter the time of application. Writing down your plans may seem tedious and superfluous, but I promise your results will increase tenfold.

The second reason for writing down your plans is to share them with others who may be able to assist you. Sometimes we don't always have time to talk in person or on the phone with someone about the details of our plans. However, if you have written, preferably typed, your plans, you can share them with people across the country in seconds, via email and or fax. This is extremely beneficial if you have a plan that requires the assistance of several people, such as applying for college scholarships. If you have prepared a detailed plan of the colleges you are hoping to attend, with the funds you have available, you can reach out for help in seconds with the click of a mouse.

The third and final reason for writing down your plans is to access the visual portion of your brain. Typed and printed plans let you see things that you never thought of when you were just storing them in your head.

OK, we know that success needs a dream and a plan but how can a person determine if he/she is doing the right amount of dreaming and planning? As we now know, success cannot be measured by a person's income or popularity but it can be measured with the imaginary life scale.

If you have hundreds of dreams a week but never create any plans, then you are probably very frustrated. Your brain is concentrating on where you want to be, but it sees that you're not there.

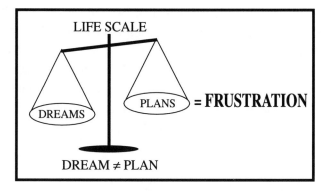

Don't worry, because you're not alone; most people daydream without creating plans. Some people have hundreds of plans a day but they lose sight of their dreams.

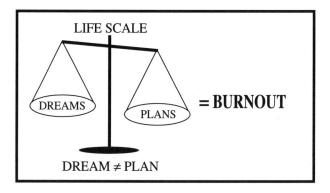

This is what is called *"Burnout."* You become so immersed in your outcome you forget what your purpose or dream was.

A simple metaphor for the "Dream/Plan balance" is fire. What does it take to create fire? A flame right? But, if you look at fire scientifically, you know that it begins with a spark. However, the spark needs oxygen and something flammable to survive. Your dreams are like sparks. They occur hundreds, if not thousands, of times a week. But unless sparks (the dream) have fuel (the plans), they die out.

Not all of your plans will work but you won't ever know until you take action on them. Remember to Think Big and put your ideas on paper; the more detailed your plans are, the better chance that your "success-flame" will burn longer and hotter. When I dreamt of this book, it seemed quite overwhelming at first. However, this book only became a reality because I created a detailed plan of how I could best spread my messages into the world. My plans didn't always work as I expected. I had to create them with enough flexibility so that each time an obstacle would occur, I could return to the drawing board and redevelop the plan.

You should not give up on your plans just because you go off course or encounter an obstacle. A sailboat heading towards a destination does not always follow a straight line. Sometimes it zigzags back and forth according to the winds but the captain always keeps the destination in mind, just as you need to keep your ultimate dream in mind. Holding all of your dreams alive from start to finish is difficult but the real test is creating master plans with enough flexibility to maneuver around the obstacles on your voyage.

Activity #5
• • • • • • • • • • •

Apply your dreams with a plan, and then take ACTION!

As I mentioned before, we all have numerous dreams in life. The question is, how can we transform them into reality? As you know, the answer is by writing out a detailed plan and then taking action.

In our first activity, you visualized what type of person you wanted to be a year from now. So now we are going to use that dream as a base for this activity. In your journal, write down all the resources you have available to you right now that could help to transform your *one-year visualization* into reality. Even though you might not take action on every single one, at least you know what you have available.

If part of your one-year visualization included a healthier body you might list,

For example:

· The school weight room and school jogging track!

· Books on nutrition in local book stores or school library!

· Walkman and music collection!

Now list in your journal ten resources that you have available in your life.

Absolutely brilliant! Knowing what you have available is important but assigning your plans to a schedule and taking action is crucial.

For example:

By tomorrow: Wake up at 7:30 AM and jog two miles and lift weights.

By next week: Check out books on nutrition and follow their suggestions.

By next month: Make a music mix to work out to.

Now seriously commit to three of your resources.

By tomorrow: (Write them down in your journal.)

By next week: (Write them down in your journal.)

By next month: (Write them down in your journal.)

Great, now take action and follow through on your commitments. I recommend you write out more resources and commitments in your journal. This will supercharge your *one-year visualization* into reality. Remember to have fun!

CHAPTER
VI

"NOTHING
BUT NET"

Skills for lifelong success!

"Nothing but Net"

Skills for lifelong success!

While exercising today, this chapter came to me in a vision. I was shooting hoops when I thought to myself, "what added hints, techniques, or strategies could I put in the book to really benefit the reader that other books often leave out?"

After pondering this thought, I started making ninety percent of the shots I threw in the bucket. My shots weren't just going in, they were making that cool "swoosh" noise that you get when you hit *nothing but net*. Then, on my last shot it hit me — no, seriously, it hit me. The ball bounced hard off the rim and came flying back towards me. I caught it right in the face. Thankfully, it didn't leave a mark, but it did leave an idea for this chapter.

Most self-help authors will share with you skills for short-term success but they leave out the skills for lifelong success. What good is learning to achieve something without being able to use and maintain it on a regular basis? That's like being told all the important tips and skills for buying a car and then leaving out how to use and maintain the car after it is purchased. Within the first week or so your car would run out of gas, without your knowing how to fill the tank, leaving you extremely frustrated. So I committed myself to writing a chapter detailing important tips that, when combined with the other skills in this book, would maintain lifelong success.

During the five minutes or so when I was hitting ninety percent of my shots, I realized the amazing similarities between shooting a ball into a hoop and lifelong success. Not even the greatest player in the world can get the ball in the hoop every time. The key is to hit more than you miss and to aim for *nothing but net*. Hitting *nothing but net* on a continual basis is a skill that surfaces only with visualization and practice.

Blending visualization and practice together creates what is known as a rhythm.

When in a rhythm, your odds of hitting *nothing but net* increase dramatically. This is because you are operating on what is known as muscle memory. Your muscles begin memorizing the physical movements it takes to gracefully hit the shot. Eventually the brain is wired for hitting *nothing but net*. You begin thinking less about the shots and more about the flow and rhythm. Success can be wired in your mind the same way.

Anyone can powerfully throw the ball against the backboard in hopes that it will go in. And, truthfully, sometimes that works but certainly not on a continual basis. The same principle holds true for success. A lifelong skill is not to strive for occasional or accidental success. This is simply too random and reckless of a technique. Instead, you should strive for greatness and brilliance. I never rely on the backboard when shooting. This is because the backboard is a safety net, and when you depend on safety nets you get careless and your successful edge becomes dull. The key is to sharpen your mind for *nothing but net* developing a rhythm for success.

Here is a set of tips for lifelong success.

TIP #1:

The Kingdom of Success is supported by four pillars.

These pillars need to be constantly reinforced and maintained. They are: **reading**, **writing**, **verbally communicating**, and **thinking**. I know it sounds very obvious but success can only be maintained if a person consistently improves these four fundamental pillars.

I. **"Reading."** There is sooooo much to read today with the Internet, Emails, magazines, books, and newspapers. There is enough reading to keep a person busy for life. Constantly reading outside of your textbooks is crucial for success, as "readers are leaders." People who maintain success in their careers, health, and relationships constantly are searching for new ideas that are presented in different forms of reading. Until I was a freshman in college, I never read for pleasure. The only time I was caught reading was for class. If I could do it all over again, I would have read more often. By not doing so, I had placed myself at a great disadvantage. New ideas are continually flowing out into the world. Yes, often these ideas are discussed on TV; however, most of the important details are left out to save time. Improving your "pillar of reading" is not about becoming a faster reader or better at reading comprehension, although those are important. To be honest, I personally am a slow reader and for years I felt discouraged to do any "outside reading." But one day I thought, "WHO CARES how slow I read!" I began forcing myself to read and, as time went on, I learned to read at my own rhythm and that is all that mattered. When you find your rhythm, then constantly skim anything you can find related to your interests and future. With outside reading, it is also important to note that not every page has to be read. If you find a book with some good ideas, just read, highlight the points of interest, then move on. Make sure you also pay attention to issues that are transpiring around the world because this impacts your future as well.

The more you know about the world you live in, the better you are equipped to succeed in it.

II. **"Writing."** What's the big deal with writing, you ask? People who can write well have a great advantage over their competitors. Now I am not hinting that you should write extra research papers for fun because school will assign you enough of those. I am talking about writing on a daily basis. The more you write, the more it will become second nature to you, like breathing. Had someone told me, when I was younger, that I would write two books by the age of 21, I would have laughed at them. Writing is very important because you can only reach so many people by speaking.

Writing is a great forum to help you spread a message.

You can capture your emotions, ideas, and opinions and then share them with hundreds of people without having to spend time talking with every individual. When I first started my inspirational business, I was nervous about writing letters and faxes to people but the more I wrote, the quicker my thoughts flowed onto the paper. A good way to become a better writer is to keep a daily journal. Most successful explorers, scientist, and authors keep daily journals. They are not just for thirteen-year-old girls to read at slumber parties. In fact, I made a promise that I would keep a journal starting with my twentieth birthday and I am glad I have kept my promise. Journals are an excellent way to record your evolution in life.

III. **"Verbally Communicating."** In college, a certain percentage of your final grade is usually class participation. So if you are uncomfortable with communicating in public then your grades may suffer in college. Does that sound unfair to you? Well, that is a fact, my friend. Increasing your communication skill is crucial for advancement in your education, career, and relationships. When I refer to communicating, I am not talking just about conversational skills, although that it is a portion of communicating. I am referring to how well you can express your message to others. Voice inflection, body language, and eye contact are the three staples of communicating.

The secret to outstanding communication is not just being comfortable with your audience, it is making sure your audience is comfortable with you.

When someone is comfortable around you, they are more inclined to help you. Take me for example. Because I am in a wheelchair and am extremely short, my appearance often makes people uncomfortable. I realize this and, instead of being angered by the fact, I just step up my communication skill. I constantly create an environment of positive energy around me. This environment comforts people to the point that they actually forget about my physical appearance.

A good way to improve your communication skill is to look at every person as a potential friend.

When you treat individuals the way you would treat a friend, they will respond in a very positive manner. So every time you meet someone tell yourself "hey, he/she is a friend."

IV. **"Thinking."** Sounds almost silly, right? Thinking, however, is a commodity most people take for granted. Most of my mistakes when I was growing up were results of not thinking, and almost all of my greatest achievements came from thinking. Thinking is a logical process of focusing your thoughts. The stronger you focus, the better the result you will receive. You've heard the saying, "knowledge is power." I feel that the

application of knowledge is power, and application is a result of thinking.

Some people say that we are always thinking, even when we sleep. So if you want to excel and succeed, you need to improve your thinking skills. Improvement comes from two things: practice and belief. If you believe that thinking is your greatest tool to survive and flourish, then you will. Practicing thinking also goes by the alias of brainstorming. If you brainstorm on paper or with your parents and friends, your success will increase exponentially. A good example of *nothing but net* success in my life would be the time I put together my public relations (PR) video. I was a junior in college and I had practically a zero budget to work with. Professional PR videos can cost $10,000 and up and I had exactly $250 in my bank account at that time. But I knew that if I did some brainstorming, I could link up all my resources and produce a really cool video.

Then one night all these ideas came flooding into my head. My brain felt like it was going to explode, it was so full of ideas. I began writing everything down as quickly as I could. My mind was sending out ideas ten times faster than my hand could write. However, I managed to get everything down. I realized in this midnight breakthrough that I could have my friend from high school, who writes music for a living, compose the score. Then I could have my neighbor's friend, who was the announcer for the Chicago Bulls, read the script for the voiceover. I also remembered a journalist friend of mine could write the script and my high school TV station could edit the final package. It all came together beautifully because I visualized my goal and then attracted the resources.

TIP #2:

Focus on where you want to go not where you are.

Life can be extremely frustrating if you are constantly upset that you haven't yet accomplished your dreams. This has certainly been my greatest struggle. Ideas are constantly flowing through my head. Then, sometimes, when I start working towards accomplishing them, I fall into the trap of focusing on where I am and not where I want to be. Whether you have been working on a project for a few hours, weeks, months, or years, it is imperative you continue to focus on your goal and not your current position. Think of this technique in terms of a road trip. When you get in your car and pull out of the driveway, do you stop the car immediately and cry because you aren't there yet? If so, please seek medical attention. My guess is you don't. In order to enjoy a road trip, you shouldn't care how long the drive is. All you need is to envision how much fun you will have when you arrive and apply that feeling every step of the way.

Embrace and enjoy the journey while envisioning your ultimate destination.

When I started exercising with my racing wheelchair, I could hardly wheel a mile without getting out of breath. For a long time, I was extremely frustrated because I could not keep up with my father who was jogging alongside of me. In addition, on the way back, I needed to be pushed because I was out of steam. I beat myself up over this. I thought there was no way I would be able to wheel faster or with more endurance. When I did this to myself, what was I doing? Yep, you guessed it, I focused on where I was instead of where I wanted to be. Just so you know, a year later I am able to wheel five miles. And the first mile can be done without limitation or hesitation.

TIP #3:

Respect yourself by maximizing your mind and body.

When you were growing up, I am sure people told you *respect this thing* or *respect that person*, but did they discuss the importance of respecting yourself? Most people view respect as something that is needed for others. Actually, respect is not just for others but, more importantly, it is for you. People will begin to respect you if you respect yourself. Self-respect is an issue your peers struggle with the most. That is why I wrote this tip.

If you could observe the people in the *Kingdom of Success*, you would witness individuals who are very secure and confident. Here is a personal question for you. Do you respect yourself? By respect, I mean do you take positive steps to improve the quality of your health and well-being? If your body could speak to your mind, what would it say? Be honest, would it say, "Please *stop* smoking, I am dying here." Or would it say, "Please exercise and stop eating *junk* food, I am exhausted."

What does your physical condition have to do with being successful? The answer is, the way you feel determines how you perform in life. Your physical condition drastically effects what you can accomplish. If you spend most of your time tired or sick, you are not in condition to climb the ladder of success. I have probably a hundred reasons why I can't exercise:

- My bones are extremely fragile and I can break them working out.
- No matter how hard I take care of my body, no one will notice because I am in a wheelchair.
- People will stare at me when I go to the gym.
- BLAH, BLAH, BLAH, etc.

Even though all those reasons are somewhat true, I still take care of my body anyway.

- work out six days a week.
- I lift weights three of the six days.
- I bench half my body weight.
- I wheel two miles almost every other day.
- I do 100 push-ups a day.
- I do 100 sit-ups a day.
- I jog on my back with weights on my legs for twenty minutes a day.
- And I follow an extremely successful way of eating.

I am not telling you this to brag. I am telling you this because I know that if I can improve my body, with all of my challenges, then you can do it, too. Taking care of your body to reach the *Kingdom of Success* doesn't just mean skipping dessert to lose a few pounds. Total fitness is not just about losing weight and toning muscle, it is about maximizing your internal energy and creating a healthy environment in which your body can thrive. Think of losing weight and gaining muscle only as nice side effects to being healthy. If you are interested in taking your body to the next level through exercise and nutritional conditioning check out my website: **www.seanstephenson.com/ health.html** OK, so we know our bodies are important instruments for success but what about the mind? Being centered and sound in mind is very important. Spend some time every-day alone without talking. Don't even play music or the TV. Even though this time alone may sound boring use it to clean out all of your limiting beliefs and replace them with empowering beliefs, as discussed in Chapter Three. Successful people feel this time alone is very important. Coach Pat Kennedy, of DePaul University, comments on this in his testimonial when he talks about Charlie Ward, who was the starting point guard at Florida State, President of the Fellowship of Christian Athletes, and Heisman Trophy winner:

"When people ask me about Charlie, I tell them, 'Charlie is one of the few young people or one of the few people in general that I know, who can sit in a room by himself and enjoy the company.' And I tell my athletes that, 'if you can enjoy the peace and company of yourself by the time you leave my program, then we have done a heck of a job.'"

Tip #4:

Real confidence is about not having to prove to others who you are.

Reach inside yourself and find what you love to do, and do it without any fear. Confidence is often confused, especially in high school and college, with cockiness. This is where humility plays an important role in your life.

Love yourself, don't be in love with yourself.

Often, people appear to be confident because they say and do things without any regard for others, but that is not confidence. A way to test if you are being confident is to ask yourself, "am I doing this to prove myself?" If the answer is yes, then you are not being confident, you are being cocky. A person can be confident without wearing it on their sleeve. Sometimes when you are confident you don't even have to speak. Confidence is stepping out of your actions and asking:

"Am I improving or just proving myself?"

My friend, Alex Henlin, is a perfect example of someone who follows this principle, as shown in this excerpt from his testimonial. He states:

"My teammates at Georgetown honored me this past spring by voting me the recipient of the Crew Spirit Award. I've been able to cross a cultural divide in Britain by projecting energy and enthusiasm to my new teammates at Oxford while taking a real interest in what interests them. I was also elected captain of my crew this past term by the seven other guys in my boat. I can't say that I'm a decent oarsman or that I am the most relaxed person you will ever meet, but I do think that I've been successful in these purely personal terms. I've had a great time in the sport; I've remained true to my principles, including collegiality in captaining, and although the work has been pretty hard in terms of making it this far, I've kept trying to become better at my chosen sport."

Alex continues to strive for improvement. He allows his actions and positive attitude to convey his confidence. He truly is a beautiful person. You also are a beautiful individual whether you realize it or not and you deserve to treat yourself with confidence. I have heard people say, "I am not a confident person." That statement is false, because confidence is not an inherited or purchased trait. It is built within every individual. Confidence exists when you say and do things that you believe in with great sincerity.

I remember a time I did something, not because I believed in it, but because I listened to my peers. When I was in grade school, three individuals teased me because I didn't listen to heavy metal music. You know there were more groups than just pop singers in the mid-1980s. When the harassment began, I just ignored these three individuals. I listened to the music I loved and didn't feel I needed to seek approval from them; that made them angry. So they made verbal attacks on me. These three guys thought that, if they put me down, then people would laugh and they would look better. Psychologically what they were really doing, in an unconscious way, was attempting to steal my confidence. Had they known that confidence was built within them, they wouldn't have been compelled to steal mine.

Sadly, these three people wore my patience down to zero. I ended up learning and memorizing all the band names and the songs so that they would think I was interested. Secretly I thought the music sounded like a bunch of mindless screaming. I wasn't following what I liked; I pretended to like what others were following.

TIP #5:

A true leader makes more leaders not more followers.

A test to see if your teacher, parent, and or coach is a good leader is to observe what happens when their students, children, and or athletes are left to work together. If total chaos breaks out, this is a sign that the mentor did not emphasize leadership enough. A "true leader" instills leadership and confidence in both their colleagues and pupils. Most of this book focuses on success as an individual goal; however, success is not completely about individuals, it is also based on groups. This tip was designed to stress the importance of cooperation as a means of success. Think of a person you enjoy being around. My guess is you like being around them because they treat you as a leader, not a follower.

A "true leader" reinforces an individual's positive attributes instead of dwelling on negative habits.

In high school, I was an officer in student council and, in college, I was a senator in the student government association on campus. In both organizations, success depended on leadership from the elected officers. Over the years of working for these organizations, I found the "true leaders" were the ones who challenged the members to lead each other. This way, if the executive officers were unable to attend a meeting, the members could congregate and run the meeting without conflict. In the military, a general's leadership is only effective if the general is alive to lead his/her troops. If the general is a "true leader" the troops stand a better chance of surviving when the general is unable to lead.

"True leaders" are not concerned with power and authority, they are more interested in accordance and progress.

TIP #6:

Individuals and groups respond better to suggestions then they do to demands.

If you are leading a group, find out what reasons motivate your members because people tend to be inspired by their reasons, not yours. You and I both have the potential to be "true leaders," it just takes patience and dedication. Controlling every decision a person makes is not truly leading, but dictating. When you are working in a group as a "true leader," you need to consider other individual viewpoints and feelings. A "true leader" recognizes that every person is filled with great ideas.

Tap into others' enthusiasm and insight and you will experience the magic of truly leading.

Tip #7:

Without sincerity, all success is empty.

Always remember that sincerity is the ability to connect with individuals at a deeper and more meaningful level. For example, take Global Youth Coach Tad Hargrave's amazing thoughts on sincerity as found in this excerpt from his testimonial:

"Sincerity isn't so much a tool or a special seed to plant in your garden of success as it is the soil itself. Even the most powerful seed cannot thrive in poor soil, just as the most powerful success tools, techniques, and skills cannot create success without sincerity."

If you want to communicate with others on a higher level, like Tad Hargrave, you need to be sincere. Sincerity is developed as much in your listening skills as it is in your speaking skills. When you ask someone a question, truly listen to their response instead of quickly thinking of the next thing you are going to say. This sign of sincerity is recognized and appreciated by almost everyone. Out of all of my *nothing but net* tips, this one makes all the others work. Treat everyone as if they were your potential best friends. If you are open and honest with your emotions, the universe will send you wonderful surprises.

Activity #6

••••••••••••

Hitting nothing but net!

Over the next seven weeks, begin integrating each of the seven tips into your life, adding a new one each week. Note your experiences in your journal so that you can document your amazing transformation. These next seven weeks are going to be merely a taste of a wonderful future. Remember that your success is equal to your commitment to hitting *nothing but net* so play full out and begin to apply the tips into your life forever.

CHAPTER
VII

SURVIVING
THE STORMS

It's not the action but the
reaction *that counts!!!*

Surviving the Storms

It's not the action but the <u>reaction</u> that counts!!!

I am not sure if you noticed but we have been on our voyage for quite some time now and we are a long way from home. You have just crossed over from being a reader to being a voyager. Prior to this point, we have sailed along the coast of reality. Now we have reached life's vast ocean of possibility. During this portion of our voyage, we will be sailing through some strong internal storms. However, before we encounter the thunder (F.E.A.R.), lightning (blame) and wind (time) let's recap the 22 main tools we have brought aboard.

● ● ● ● ● ● ● ● ● ● ● ●

1. Every decision we make determines the future of our individual destiny!

2. Geniuses study the obvious!

3. The stronger your visualization, the faster you will accomplish your outcome!

4. What you think transfers into what you say. What you say transfers into what you do.

5. You can be a *master* of your thoughts or a *servant* to them.

6. All of the positive thoughts and words in the world are useless without taking action.

7. Tools and strategies won't help you if you don't believe in them or yourself.

8. Every individual, including yourself, has the potential to achieve all that is believed.

9. Your personal capabilities are only as strong or weak as your lenses of belief.

10. If you think you can or you think you can't, you're right!

11. Set yourself free from can't and you will enter the *Kingdom of Success*.

12. Combine your dreams with a plan and then take action!

13. Success has very little to do with possessions and a lot to do with improvement.

14. Clarity = Power!

15. Reading, Writing, Communicating, and Thinking are the pillars to success!

16. Focus on where you want to go, not where you are.

17. Successful people respect what they have, including their minds and their bodies.

18. Real confidence is about *not* having to prove to others who you are.

19. Love yourself, don't be in love with yourself.

20. A true leader makes more leaders, not more followers.

21. True leaders reinforce positive attributes instead of dwelling on negative habits.

22. Individuals and groups respond better to suggestions then to demands.

• • • • • • • • • • • • •

Now that we have gathered an outstanding inventory of tools and strategies, we are prepared to endure the storms. If success were a calm voyage, everyone would join us. Unfortunately, success is not achieved without the eventual appearance of internal and external storms. Internal storms are self-generated turbulent emotions that are created completely out of imagination such as fear, blame, and procrastination. External storms are those unavoidable and likely unforeseen incidents such as the death of a loved one, parental divorce, or personal injuries. It seems just when everything is going well, BANG, life presents you with an external storm like the one Sean Graves experienced when he was shot at Columbine High School on April 20, 1999. In this excerpt from his testimonial, Sean writes:

"I'm right now working on how to walk again. I am hoping to have a full recovery. As for Lance, he is working hard with many surgeries to get his face back. I am currently back at school. Lance and I both decided to return to Columbine High School, as did the others affected directly. I am not sure as to why, except we survived and prevailed."

Because you can't control external storms, I recommend that you overcome your internal ones, as Sean Graves has. This way you have the energy and mental sanity to deal with your external storms.

Thunderous Fear

This chapter was designed to calm a few of the many internal storms in your life. Let's begin by looking at the thunderous fear. What is thunder? It is merely the noise made during a storm because of clouds, atmosphere, etc. It is completely harmless, yet its booms, cracks, and loud rumbles can make you feel scared and insecure. In actuality, it is nothing more than a sound. To my knowledge, no one was ever killed by thunder. Fear, like thunder, is merely a warning. During my junior year of college at DePaul University, I learned in a childhood development course that fear is a socially constructed concept. We human beings are born with only two fears, heights and loud noises; the rest of fear is fabricated by our perception of reality. Therefore, fear is an imaginary concept constructed in our own personal reality. I believe fear is an acronym for:

False
Experiences
Appearing
Real

Most of what we fear never comes to pass yet we still spend hours of our time channeling our fear into worry. For example, a few months ago I had two teeth pulled to leave room for my wisdom teeth. I admit I spent a ridiculous amount of time visualizing false experiences. I made these false experiences appear so vivid that I began to believe they were real. When I had my teeth pulled they didn't even hurt. I truly created a racket of thunderous fear for nothing. The fear I had created was a hundred billion times worse than what actually came about. If you fabricate hundreds of false experiences into your reality, you will become prisoner of your fabrications. The good news is, like thunder, fear is a warning device. When fear enters your mindset, you are forced to sharpen your awareness and hone your reactions. When you begin to fear something, do not retreat, instead simply step up the quality of your reactions to avoid the dangerous lightning also known as blame.

Lightning – Blame

If you pay attention to the warning signs of F.E.A.R., than you can avoid being struck by lightning — blame. In life, there are two outlooks an individual can hold regarding his/her ability to succeed. Some individuals blame their success and failure on their individual life choices. This outlook is achieved only from the acceptance of personal responsibility. Other individuals blame their level of success or failures strictly on their environment (economic level, geographic location, disability, family, etc.). Life, however, is not that black and white. Success is achieved in the gray areas. The environment you are born into heavily "influences" your situation but it does not impact it indefinitely or eternally.

Life can be unpredictable at times. If you want to succeed in any situation always keep this in mind,

The only thing you have absolute control over is your attitude and emotions. So embrace the fact that it's not the actions but the reactions that matter.

Friends, family, and love interests will come and go but your emotions will be with you until the grave. You may blame other people and situations for your anger, depression, and or hatred but, in the end, only you decide the emotions you want to experience.

Have you ever said, "That person makes me so angry?" Technically, you made yourself angry because of something they did or didn't do. We are programmed in this society to blame our emotions on outside influences, as if our emotions are a separate body part, independent of our control. This belief is completely **false**! And like lightning, this external blame is also one of the most destructive forces present on earth.

Unfortunately, this destructive force has been indoctrinated in most everyone's set of beliefs. This belief falsely excuses people from feeling any responsibility over their emotions. Success follows the same patterns and principles as your emotions. If you plan your happiness around other people and the situations beyond your control, you are probably frustrated most of the time. Take, for example, those who blame their attitude on the weather. If they live in a city with changing seasons, they can only be happy a few months of the year. This is why I create my own emotional weather. Emotional weather is a mental strategy used to create a constant feeling of joy. I close my eyes and focus on a warm spring day in May. I imagine the sound of birds chirping, the smell of fresh-cut grass, and the feeling of the sun painting my entire body as I stroll through the park.

Unfortunately, most people blame their emotions on what happens to them in life. If I did this, I would have been in my room crying for over two decades of my life. Living with my disorder has not been easy for my family or me. As I previously mentioned my disorder affects the growth and brittleness of my bones. I have broken them over 200 times in my life. Something as simple as sneezing has fractured my collarbone.

I had to sit back as a kid and watch my friends go outside and play sports; in high school, not much changed. All I could do was watch them rush out and get their drivers' licenses, leaving me again to entertain myself. While other kids cried because they broke a nail, I cried because I broke two ribs and an arm. I could have found thousands of reasons to feel sorry for myself, *but I didn't*! I realized that my disability was a gift, not a burden.

Did you know that when lightning is directed into the ground, it revitalizes the earth's soil? When I realized that blame operated similarly, I was able to harness the lightning in my life by taking responsibility for my own emotions, creating an unstoppable force of energy.

Winds of Time

Wind, like time, is an invisible yet powerful force. If wind is not directed properly into your sails, it will blow you in every which direction without allowing you to stay on a certain course toward a particular destination. This disorganized sailing technique is similar to the misdirection of time, otherwise known as procrastination. When you begin to procrastinate, you let your time blow you around in a disorganized fashion, never really charting your dreams on a course to reality. When you follow this strategy in life, you become preoccupied with any and every distraction that passes by.

I know this from first-hand experience. Whenever I would have a paper due during my freshman year of college, I would set aside a day to work on it. However, when that day arrived, I would begin searching out every little distraction that I deemed important, like checking my email ten times an hour or reorganizing my computer desktop. When you are procrastinating, you are allowing your sails to flap freely without any direction. Even though you may appear busy checking your email, you are not letting the winds of time assist you in reaching your ultimate destination.

Someone who sails through life, not using their winds of time properly, will never transform their dreams into reality. If you ask a person who is not harnessing their winds of time when they are going to resolve their internal conflicts and take control of their life, their response is "maybe in the future." People who procrastinate act as if the future is an island where tasks become easier to accomplish. This grants them the ability to never take steps towards improving the present. Are you one of these people? Do you put off dealing with your lack of self-esteem, identity confusion, or bottled-up rage in hopes that, when you arrive at that island, everything will be resolved? If you answered yes, then I am quite certain you have constant internal battles and this pain has been festering inside you for years. If so, do you put important things in your life like taking care of your health onto this island called "the future?"

...WARNING: The follow passage could change your life forever...

It is crucial that you *cease* procrastination and take action *now* to improve yourself. If you continue lying to yourself about how things will get better without changing your attitude and lifestyle, eventually the storms may be so turbulent you won't be able to find the island.

The only time is NOW!

NOW is yesterday's *future* so stop misusing the winds of time or your dreams will never be fulfilled in *your future.*

In closing...

Now that you are aware of the three elements to an internal storm, thunder (F.E.A.R.), lightning (blame), and wind (time), you can survive and succeed in life. A sophisticated life voyager acknowledges that storms inevitably arise in life and they prepare for them by following one rule: It is not the size or the strength of the storms but how you handle them that determines your survival. People and society may give you a million reasons why you are not capable of succeeding. But they are not the ones molding your destiny, *you are!*

Be prepared for any thunder, lightning, and wind. If you believe you will survive the storms, you will. When storms grow strong, just rely on what you've learned here. Live life with energy every day and take care of your body because it is your only vessel in this life. Take care of yourself by becoming one of your own best friends. Make sure to avoid negative and destructive environments at all cost. Enjoy and appreciate the good times and the challenging times because you can learn from them both. True success and total fulfillment arrive only when you contribute to the lives of others as well as your own.

Your life can be so amazing if you pull up your anchors of negativity, raise your sails of opportunity, and sail into the Kingdom of Success.

You are the reason why I wrote this book. So I have confidence that, if you follow the strategies I put together, you will begin to transform your dreams into reality by living a life of phenomenal success and happiness. First and foremost, have faith that you can improve the world by first improving yourself! When you have this confidence, life is a giant jungle gym, where you can swing freely from every situation (both good and bad) that occurs. I hope to meet you someday at one of my speeches or seminars. I look forward to seeing you in the *Kingdom of Success*; until then, go forth and be brilliant, my friend!

Activity #7
• • • • • • • • • • •
Enjoy and apply!

Congratulations! You made it. Now your only activity is to read and apply the knowledge from the amazing individual testimonials found on the following pages...ENJOY!

PERSONAL
RECIPES FOR SUCCESS

SURVIVE AND PREVAIL

Sean Graves ~ Student at Columbine High School

My name is Sean Graves. I am a sixteen-year-old sophomore at Columbine High School. I was shot on April 20th, 1999. I was with my friends, Lance Kirkland and Dan Roughbogh. My friends and I would do our typical ritual everyday finish lunch, and then go outside so that Lance could smoke a cigarette. That day started out as being a normal day. We would bore ourselves with the morning periods and look forward to lunch. That lunch is one that I will never forget.

We sat down for a typical lunch; only for some reason, we didn't eat. We just sat and talked. I spilled Dan's pop on his lap, causing a great need for leaving the commons area early. I don't blame myself, for that it was an accident and we didn't know what was going to happen next. Lance, being the typical teenager with an edge for cigarettes, suggested we all leave early so Dan could air out his pants. As we left the commons, we started up a hill just outside the door to notice two seniors dressed in black loading what looked to be realistic paint ball guns. We were soon proven wrong after Dylan Klebold and Eric Harris opened fire on Richard Castoldo and Rachelle Scott. Once they began shooting, we stopped walking and tried to figure out what they were doing. Between the three of us, we came to the conclusion that they were cap guns and were part of the senior game, "Annihilation." Dylan shot Dan first and moved to Lance. I was the last standing and looking around for the paint balls that we all assumed they were shooting. I was shot three times in the abdomen and grazed once in the neck before I decided to turn and run. I had made it back to the door to the commons area and was going through before I was shot in the back, taking the legs out from underneath me. I lay in the doorway while the two shooters killed my friend Dan and blew my friend Lance's face off. I don't know why I was left in the doorway alive. It was an act of God. The reality of being shot didn't sink in until after the killers moved to the library. I had seen my blood and was getting cold from the loss of it. I had propped the door open to the commons area with my backpack and was looking around for other victims. I peeked around the corner where Lance and Dan were. I could see that Lance was bleeding from the mouth and Dan's leg's were motionless. The killers returned to the commons area and were setting off pipe bombs and screaming words I couldn't understand. They had returned back to the library while Lance and I became unconscious. Towards the end, before being picked up by the medical team, I was getting quite tired and I remember being dragged to the ambulance while Dylan and Eric were firing at the medical technicians from the library windows. I looked over to see that my friend Dan had turned blue and was no longer alive. They (the medical technicians) put Lance on top of me until they could get out of the line of fire.

I spent a good month at Swedish Medical Center until I was transferred to Craig Rehabilitation Center. At Swedish I was in the Intensive Care Unit for a week or so. I was unconscious most of my stay until I got to MTU (Multi Trauma Unit). I was in quite a lot of pain for the entire stay at Swedish Hospital. Because of my injury being "incomplete" my nerves were starting back up, causing my legs to be very sensitive to the touch, and were extremely painful. I graduated to Craig Rehabilitation Center where I took on working with what muscles, I had to get them stronger again. Everyday I would start with intense physical therapy before I would move on to learning new life lessons. I spent almost three months learning how to live on my own again.

I'm right now working on how to walk again. I am hoping to have a full recovery. As for Lance, he is working hard with many surgeries to get his face back. I am currently back at school. Lance and I both decided to return to Columbine High School, as did the others affected directly. I am not sure as to why, except we survived and prevailed.

Columbine High School has changed a bit since April 20, with more security and friendly faces. People don't really talk to me because I think they don't know what to say. I am trying to do my best to fit in and be one of the guys. It can be hard sometimes, knowing people are looking at you and you're one of the few to be in a wheelchair, one of the few to survive being shot April 20 at Columbine High School.

I don't look at people in wheelchairs the same way I used to. I would look at them and be sad for them before, but now I look and think how lucky they are to be here. I respect people in wheelchairs now. In the future I will do my best to help people, using my experience for the good. Thank you for reading this.

LESSONS OF STRUGGLE

Jaime Alanis Guajardo ~ Instructor at DePaul University

I have a story to tell about my magical life and the meaning of struggle. My parents entered Chicago via a traditional Mexican working class port, "Little Village." This is where I grew up for the first five years of my life. It was here where I first experienced, but did not fully comprehend poverty. I used to think that all neighborhoods had huge rats in the alley. I also imagined that every household was occupied with cockroaches. The apartment which we dubbed "La Casa Chiquita," or "The Little House," was so small that there were only two rooms; the living room literally ran into the kitchen. The neighborhood was characterized by street gangs, drugs, and violence. Street fights were a common occurrence to be in and to be witnessed by many kids in the neighborhood.

One day, my parents decided to move to another neighborhood; Humboldt Park. Throughout the 1970s, Humboldt Park was considered one of the most dangerous "barrios" or neighborhoods in the country; the homicide rate, along with the population density for this community, was disproportionately high. As it was, the move turned out to be from the Near West ghetto to the Northwest ghetto. This new ghetto represented further challenges for survival. The apartment was strategically located so that we ended up being surrounded by numerous rival street gangs.

One of the ways that we spent much of our free time was by playing sports. However, it would be a great simplification to suggest that these activities kept us out of trouble. Forever present were the dangers of every ghetto: physical segregation, poverty, drugs, police brutality, street gang violence, and despair. For my brother and me, sports turned out to be a key to receiving a certain amount of respect from our peers in the neighborhood, which granted us protection for being ball players. The other side of survival entailed dodging bullets, or just old plain luck if one lacks faith in God. There were many days when I was almost shot, where a bullet only grazed or buzzed by me. Many friends and acquaintances were not so fortunate. Death was an everyday reality in the ghetto. Many people I knew from the neighborhood ended up dead or in prison.

During the summer, my parents used to take us to Monterrey, Mexico, for vacation. It was there where I started dreaming of a different life. For the first time in my life, I saw people of my racial background in professional positions. I saw Mexicans who were doctors, lawyers, business people, police officers, and this inspired me. I began to compare differences between life in Mexico and life in the U.S. ghetto. It was then that I began to imagine a better future for myself. I began to see that people of my background could make it if given the opportunity. This was a moment of self-affirmation for me. Pride in my culture sparked a seed of hope inside me. I realized that maybe there was a way out of the ghetto.

In high school, I made the basketball team, worked after school to pay for tuition, and kept my grades up. During my senior year in high school, I took the ACT test and scored a whopping thirteen. I spoke with my school counselor and he asked me, "Are you good with your hands?" I said, "Not really." He responded by informing me that I had the option of attending a community college and that perhaps after two years, I could transfer to a four-year university. I decided to take this option.

While attending the community college, I associated myself with the wrong crowd. I used to cut class, party heavily almost every weekend, smoke weed, and hang out with my girlfriend very frequently. As a result of this, I received low grades and generally did not learn much. My older brother, who is my best friend, witnessed the trouble I had gotten myself into, so he advised me to join the Marine Corps Reserves and transfer to DePaul University. My brother's advice was that I needed to get away from the bad influences at the community college.

I went to boot camp in San Diego and completed my military occupational specialty in six months. During those six months, I had much time to think and make sense about things back home in Chicago. I realized that most of the people around me were influencing me negatively. I also thought about how I was being distracted and how much of my energy was being wasted. I began to realize that I needed to bring myself around positive people, people I could learn from. I thought about how everyone around me was taking from me but not giving. I recognized for the first time that the folks I chose to spend time with were bringing me down and holding my potential back.

After my return from Camp Pendleton, California, I transferred to DePaul University. My first semester, I was put on academic probation. At first, I was a bit surprised at the academic expectations but soon adjusted well with some tutoring and guidance from my older brother. Gradually, my writing and critical thinking skills increased and consequently, my grades went up.

When I started senior year, my mentor highly recommended that I attend graduate school. At first, I thought he was just trying to boost my ego. When he insisted that he would assist me in the process of applying, I knew he was serious. I had great doubts about my chances of getting accepted since my grade point average was not as high as the requirements stipulated. My mentor decided to intervene in the process and vouch for me. I was finally accepted on a probationary basis. I had to prove that I was up to the academic standards of graduate school. At this point, I was hungry for knowledge, I was devouring books and articles like there was no tomorrow. I wanted to know the secrets of the universe. It took me five years to complete a study on street gangs that served as my master's thesis. When I submitted it to the chair of the Department of Sociology, he asked me if I would be interested in teaching an introductory course in sociology. I now teach introduction to sociology to students and continue to work with and mentor youth in the Little Village community.

I would like to give a few words of humble advice to young people. You are going through difficult times. It is not easy for you. Be a chess player in life. In chess, you always have to be two moves ahead, or your king will end up getting trapped. In life, checkmate is when you end up in prison. Don't get caught up in life's traps. Love yourself. Don't allow the venom of self-hatred to enter your veins. Place yourself around positive people, people who are going to push you to grow as a person. Look for *one* professional adult whom you admire. Ask them to mentor you. Seek your mentors, bother them, learn from them, hang out and ask them many questions. Choose your friends carefully. You have to surround yourself with good people and the good "karma" will rub off. Stay strong, keep struggling, keep dreaming, follow your heart, and keep hope alive. You have a tremendous challenge in life and must keep the words of the late Frederick Douglas in mind. "Without struggle, there is no progress."

SINCERITY = SUCCESS

Tad Hargrave ~ Global Youth Coach

*"Who you are shouts so loudly in my ears that
I can not hear what you are saying."*

– Emerson

When Sean asked me to come up with a story to illustrate the power of sincerity to create success from my life, I had a hard time–a sincerely hard time. Sincerity isn't so much a tool or a special seed to plant in your garden of success as it is the soil itself. Even the most powerful seed cannot thrive in poor soil, just as the most powerful success tools, techniques, and skills cannot create success without sincerity. Sincerity makes every other quality work.

The reason that Sean asked me to write this was because he felt I was sincere. Think about that. I didn't ask him if I could, he asked me. When you become sincere, you will attract amazing opportunities rather than you having to hunt them down. Sincerity is about two things: desires and action. I was, for the first time in my life, taking a major risk to follow a sincere desire I had. You know it's a sincere desire when you can't get rid of it. It just keeps bubbling up.

For me, it was going to Hawaii, not just to tan but to attend a leadership seminar. I was eighteen, fresh out of high school, and I had a small problem. It cost $6,000 not including airfare, food or a place to stay. After raising enough money for the airfare, I immediately bought a ticket and flew to Hawaii, convinced I would meet someone at the event who would loan me the remaining $6,000 or so. I had no place to stay and very little money for food. So I started asking people for money. After being rejected dozens of times, I sat next to a man I knew and said, "Listen. I'm either really stupid or really brave, but I have to be in that event. This isn't your problem. You don't need to help me, but if you do, I swear I'll pay you back. I swear on my soul." He said yes. The next ten days of the event changed my life forever and shaped the course of my destiny.

Looking back, I realize that sincere desires gain their truest power in action. Sincere desires, when acted upon, create miracles. My desire to be at the event was genuine and so were my actions. People tend not to loan you $6,000 on the spot if they don't feel you are sincere.

As a direct result of my experience at that event, I have spoken to, and worked with, youth from over eighty countries around the world, founded one of the world's leading annual gatherings for young leaders, and met many incredible authors, celebrities, and business leaders who are beyond the reach of most people. I can honestly say that the number one reason is sincerity. The higher up you go, the less techniques you need and the more sincerity. Successful people have very little time to waste on people with hidden agendas or shifty eyes. They smell a lack of honesty immediately. When they meet someone who is focused and sincere, they are often taken aback because all too often, they are worshiped—which, I might add, is not a form of sincerity. Just as you can't fake good soil and trick the seeds, you can't fake sincerity.

Make peace of mind your only goal every day. This is the core principle and measuring stick of sincerity. Want to check if you were sincere? Take a few minutes alone and review a situation in your life. See how you acted and reacted, and ask yourself, "Was I sincere? Did I hold back? Hide the truth?" And then notice how you feel. If you feel a wave of peace and calm, then you were sincere. If not, that's a great signal from your body to take a look at the principles below and see where you are off course.

What you do not say communicates far more powerfully than what you do say. Transparency means that people can see right through you. It means that you have no hidden agenda or secret motives. This is hard to do, but the closer you get, the more at peace you will feel, and you will be amazed how quickly other people pick up on it.

Say what you mean and mean what you say. People, while trusting by nature, are very perceptive and can spot any hint of insincerity or lack of credibility. How can you share your feelings if you don't know what they are? How can you speak from a sincere place if you don't trust it? It's pretty difficult to be sincere if you don't trust your own emotional signals. Sometimes people will feel tension or uncertainty about a decision and decide to ignore it and then suffer later. Remember, peace of mind is your only goal. We are often blind to our own faults and inconsistencies. Sometimes we don't ever notice that we have a hidden agenda or that we are manipulating others until someone tells us.

ABSOLUTE SUCCESS

Alex Henlin ~ Captain of the Oxford University crew team

I'm not going to try to convince you that success is easy to achieve, that you will earn fabulous rewards if you stick to a task with single-minded devotion, or that you will necessarily be happy as long as you're on your way to reaching your goal. How could I? Success is a notoriously hard thing to achieve. Material rewards do not always follow your set course of action.

Realizing your goal and thereby achieving success in the world of human affairs might not even bring you the satisfaction that you thought it would when you began.

I'm convinced that there are two types of success, one of which is far more meaningful and relevant to quality of life than the other. The first is relative success: we look at a person's achievements, material possessions, and accomplishments and then judge him/her a success (or failure) according to where they place in society at large. Let's look at me. I captained my high school debate team for two years. I went off to the elite Boys Nation program run by the American Legion. I graduated from my high school as valedictorian. And I was fortunate enough to gain a year-long grant to study history and politics at Oxford in the United Kingdom during my junior year at university. By some estimates, I've been successful. I've been able to distinguish myself from my peers by doing things that they have not done. The problem with this view is that I do not consider myself to have been terribly deserving of the term "successful." In my own mind, I've only done what anyone else in my position would have done. I made the best possible decisions for my life when I needed to make them. Luck has played a large role in getting me where I am today, and it would be wrong for me to play up my own achievements for the sake of gaining recognition by human society.

Far more important than relative success is absolute success — the sort of satisfaction you get from knowing that you've done your job well and through your own hard work. For instance, would you consider Mother Theresa to have been a successful person or a failure? Would you call Ghandi or Martin Luther King, Jr. successful, or would you term them failures as well? What is it about these people that allowed them to achieve notoriety and success? And, most important of all, what lessons can we learn from their examples?

To throw one more example at you, I've loved the sport of rowing ever since I started my freshman year at Georgetown

University in 1997. I went out for crew, not really knowing what to expect. I'd never been terribly athletic. I'd been in debate for four years in high school, and I wasn't all that sure how I would relate to the other people who came out for my team. I resolved from early on that I would be energetic, positive, and willing to adapt, based on what my coach and my teammates told me, in essence, that I would be a good team player. If I hadn't made that decision, then I very well could have failed in my quest to experience crew. Fortunately for me, that never happened.

Three years later, as I find myself at Oxford, that training and active decision making has paid off. My teammates at Georgetown honored me this past spring by voting me the recipient of the Crew Spirit Award. I've been able to cross a cultural divide in Britain by projecting energy and enthusiasm to my new teammates at Oxford while taking a real interest in what interests them. I was also elected captain of my crew this past term by the seven other guys in my boat. I can't say that I'm a decent oarsman or that I am the most relaxed person you will ever meet, but I do think that I've been successful in these purely personal terms. I've had a great time in the sport; I've remained true to my principles, including collegiality in captaining, and although the work has been pretty hard in terms of making it this far, I've kept trying to become better at my chosen sport.

Success isn't easy. It takes hard work, usually very hard work, to make anything worthwhile happen, and it can be a real test of personal mettle to make an unpleasant decision while remaining true to your principles. However, even though it is hard, I'm convinced that everyone can be an absolute success. We can't all be relatively more successful than our neighbors, but we can achieve success on our own terms. If your dream is to succeed, whether you measure that as going to Oxford, winning a spot on a professional sports team, or devoting your life to service through charity or church you can succeed on your own effort and on your own terms. Regardless of what anyone tells me, I am convinced, on the basis of my own experience that belief in yourself is the first, and the most necessary, step on the road to success of any sort.

FINDING A PEACE OF MIND AND HEART

Patrick Kennedy ~ Head Coach of DePaul University's basketball team

Unlike most basketball coaches who start by coaching high school ball, I went straight to college coaching. When I was twenty-three years old, I was a division one full time assistant. I got into coaching because my father owned a summer basketball camp that coached kids ten to eighteen years old. So when I was in high school I was coaching during my summers. So for ten consecutive summers, I worked for twelve straight weeks with kids. And over the years, I have continued to run summer camps across the country in conjunction with the universities I coach for. Most of what people see coaches do is working with the alumni and media. However, the majority of my day, approximately — 85% to 90% is spent with young adults. I am forty-eight-years old and happily married with three kids. My greatest pleasure as a coach is helping kids working through their problems off the court. I tell people that the greatest thing a coach can do is to help the individual athlete by helping them to find a peace of mind and a peace of heart.

For example, I had the pleasure of working with Charlie Ward who won the Heisman Trophy and who was also the starting point guard at Florida State, President of the Fellowship of Christian Athletes and a legitimate Fellowship Christian athlete, who carried a 3.0 or 3.2 G.P.A. When people ask me about Charlie, I tell them, "Charlie is one of the few young people or one of the few people in general that I know, who can sit in a room by himself and enjoy the company." And I tell my athletes that, "if you can enjoy the peace and company of yourself by the time you leave my program, then we have done a heck of a job." Charlie had such peace of mind and heart from his faith and his family. But for me as a coach, there are tangible ways I can help people find peace of heart and peace of mind. For example, say you have a player who has a father at home who is physically abusing his mother. When that kid comes to practice, I can tell his stomach is in knots. I can tell maybe I can't solve his problem but I can help by just acknowledging that I see he has one. By bringing him in and talking about it, letting the kid open up and unleash his emotions. By letting him cry or releasing his frustrations by banging on my desk when he leaves, he has found some way of releasing his tension, which relieves part of the problem itself. My job as a coach has always been to learn how to relieve the pressures and anxiety from the lives of my athletes, because no one operates well when his or her sanity is threatened. If a person is emotionally and physically distraught, you won't get any performance out any of them. So what I tell young adults is that if they want to reach the goal of *peace of mind* and a *peace of heart,* they need to find a mentor. In fact, it is impossible to do it alone, you must find a mentor, whether it is a parent, teacher, counselor, coach, or friend you can really share things with. That individual must be older than your peers. You have to find someone who has already gone through what you are experiencing. Maybe this is an older aunt, uncle, or neighbor. However, it must be someone you trust and can turn to with honest and open discussion. To find this mentor, there is no exact science because your selection depends on how you feel when you are around this person. Who knows how this mentor may enter into your life, but it needs to be someone you are not threatened by. After you find this mentor use him or her as a resource for avoiding painful situations they may have experienced. There is no need for suffering that can be avoided by a few friendly words of advice from a mentor.

In closing I want to say that if you feel the world is against you, or that you are the only one experiencing frustration, simply count your blessings. Look at all the little things in your life that you can be grateful for. You will be surprised if you listed on paper all the small things that you are blessed with, such as a close parent or friend, good health, receiving an education, or certain talents. The world is a wonderful place if you allow it to be.

"NEVER HAVE TO SAY – I WISH I WOULD HAVE..."

Kary Odiatu ~ Ms. Fitness Universe

It was during my university years that my life changed dramatically. My hobbies in the past had been parties and boys, but I started to realize that if I was going to be an outstanding role model, I needed to demand more from myself. Enough of the "if only I would have!" I headed for the weight room, determined to become fit. I'll never forget that first day of training. I was the only girl in a room full of sweaty, heaving muscle; I just wanted to turn and run. I had a weightlifting friend show me the ropes and I soon forgot about my status in the gym — I was hooked. I began reading every book and magazine that I could find on fitness. I started running around the track, battling my asthma with every step. It took a long time before I was able to run a mile without stopping, but I eventually did it!

When I began competing in women's fitness, I dreamed of world-class competition. I also knew that a dream could become a reality if you believe in yourself and move with urgency toward your goals. In my eyes, a successful person is one who strives for continuous self-improvement and growth, never looking back and saying, "I wish I would have. . .!" When you live your life with this attitude, each day is like an adventure, and you have complete authority over the outcomes for your success.

My fitness universe adventure started when I won the Canadian title and earned a spot to compete on the Canadian team, which was headed for Greece for the Ms. Fitness Olympia and then to Vegas for the Ms. Fitness Universe. I was excited to see Greece, but I had my heart set on winning the Universe title. This would not be an easy task, as some of the best competitors in the World were thinking the same thing!

It takes a lot of hard work to prepare for a fitness contest. I trained between two to four hours per day, six days a week! My training consisted of dance, gymnastics, weight training, cardiovascular training, flexibility training, and routine work. During this time I also had to monitor exactly what I was eating so that my body would get the best nutrition possible. I kept a journal every day to record all of my training information, and I used visualization to build my confidence. I practiced perfectly in my mind, and this greatly improved my performance. At this level of competition, you will not succeed if you do not believe that you are a winner!

I placed third in Greece, and it would have been easy for me to just give up my desire to win the universe title because I knew that I would have to perform better than the two girls who had placed ahead of me if I wanted to win! I worked hard on my routine and used the third-place finish in Greece and my desire to better it as motivation to push through the physical exhaustion that I was feeling from all of the traveling and training. I knew that I had to be better than I ever had been before. I focused all my attention on being a winner and doing the best job possible. I thought about all of the hard work and effort I had put into this sport over the last four years. I knew that I could not just give up because I did not win the last contest!

I competed with confidence and pride at the Ms. Fitness Universe and I knew deep in my heart that I was a winner, no matter what the outcome, because I had done my best. I was rewarded for my efforts and my faith with the world-class title that I had dreamed about from the first day that I started competing. The universe title became mine that day, but that is not the most amazing thing about my story. You see, I grew up in a small town of 13,000 people, and I did not play any sports outside of gym class as a teenager! I had a big dream to be a successful athlete, and I made it happen. I truly believe that the only limits we have in life are those that we set upon ourselves!